FOR THOSE TEARS

FOR THOSE TEARS

by
Nora Lam
and
Cliff Dudley

NEW LEAF PRESS

Harrison, Arkansas

All biblical quotations are taken with permission from the *New American Standard Bible*, (C) The. Lockman Foundation, La Habra, California.

ISBN   0-88419-058-7

Library of Congress Catalog
Card Number: 72-85413

Table of Contents

Chapter One
THE JOURNEY

The train station was so crowded that I forgot the rags I was wearing; I forgot about the dirt that was smeared on my face. I could only stand and stare at the hundreds of bodies pushing and shoving about me, their faces never looking down to see an eleven-year-old girl who was dressed as a beggar for the first time in her life.

But I was glad to be leaving Shanghai with my parents. It might mean tears to my mother, and anger to my father at having to leave all his property to the Japanese, but the only thing

I could think of was that I was getting away from my grandmother. I was leaving her house, that dark, ancient building where the eyes of Buddhas were always piercing into you, in whatever room you went, and where preserved meat hung in the halls, rotten and stinking, casting dark, ominous shadows. I was leaving all that behind, and I was going to see people. Even the crush of the bodies about me was welcome. They were people, real flesh-and-blood human beings.

But their faces did not look so human now. They were pushing, clawing, screaming, trying to get a place on the train, hoping to somehow escape the madness of the Japanese soldiers. I was being pushed and shoved along with the crowd when a sudden fear clutched my heart. I felt terribly alone, and I jerked my head around in all directions. My parents were gone! I couldn't see them anywhere!

I panicked, darting between people, pushing and shoving, looking everywhere for them. But what could I do? I couldn't see over the people in the crowd, and there were hundreds and hundreds of milling people.

"God, help me," I cried. "Don't let them leave without me! God, please help me!"

I didn't feel ashamed that the only time I ever spoke to God was when I was desperate. I didn't know enough to be ashamed. I just kept crying out to my new friend, as I searched through the crowd of people intent on finding their spot on the train.

And then I saw them, standing out of the crowd, looking for me. I ran to them. "Mother, Mother, don't leave me. I'm here," I screamed, and I ran into her arms. I buried my face in her clothes. What a relief I felt! My parents had waited for me. And this new God—He really did hear prayers! He was alive! He was different from the Buddhas, made of stone and clay.

We jammed our way onto the train. There was hardly room. The seats were full, the aisles were full, people were packed so close together that it was impossible to fall down, even when the train lurched out of the station. I kept my hand clutched tightly in my mother's. The train got hot. It had the potent, repulsive smell of people who are scared and packed tightly together. The heat became overpowering. Some of the women fainted, but there was no place to lay them down. Their limp bodies had to be held between their friends. Their heads wagged back and forth with the movement of the train, and their faces turned into white masks.

It was a horrible experience. The trip to Nanking took eight hours. There was no food, no water, no means of sanitation. The stench got worse and worse. And yet I was glad. With every mile we went I was farther from the cruel Japanese, and from my grandmother and the Buddha eyes that followed you across a room.

I never thought that I could last eight hours. The rags I was wearing chafed, and were slick with sweat. I would get faint and see the world closing with blackness to the size of a train tunnel. But somehow the time passed.

When the train pulled slowly into the station at Nanking I heard a groan from my parents. "What is it?" I asked, but they didn't answer. I wiggled my way to the window. There were soldiers outside, standing watching the train come in—Japanese soldiers, dressed in the uniform that I had learned to hate, wearing cruel, calm faces.

They searched the train before we could leave. They opened what things we had brought and strewed them out on the ground beside the train. We stood and watched as they took watches, pens, flashlights and whatever else they could find of value. We looked like beggars, and we had possessions of beggars, so they let us go.

As we walked away I heard screams, and I couldn't help turning to look back. I stood staring. The soldiers were pulling some of the women away, I didn't know to where. One woman I remember was doing all the screaming, and was clutching at her husband. One of the soldiers grabbed her fiercely and made her kneel down. He took his bayonet from his side and, in one vicious chop, he cut her head off. She went limp and toppled into a pool of her own blood.

Another soldier was approaching a pretty young woman clutching a baby. She looked terrified, and she was holding the baby close to her. The soldier wrenched it out of her arms, tossed it up in the air, a tiny baby, and caught it on the tip of his bayonet.

I was standing frozen still, and suddenly I felt my father's hand jerking me around. "Walk," he hissed. "Walk and don't look."

There were twenty-seven in our group. About eight hours after our arrival in Nanking we regathered outside the city. Our long walk began. During the daylight hours we hid in bushes and behind trees, and then at night we would walk or run with the hope of escaping. About this time we realized how important it was to have good shoes, for the old ones we had were soon worn out on the bottom. We walked and stumbled over rugged paths and mountain trails. Soon my feet were sore and bleeding. So that I could walk, my mother took an old shirt and wrapped it around my feet as shoes. How good they felt! None of us had realized how awful this trip would be. Thank God! He only lets us know what life will be moment by moment. However, we kept thinking of freedom, away from the eyes of the Japanese. This hope kept us going.

Our food consisted of black buns, or whatever we could buy along the way with the small amount of money we had left. The food we could afford to buy was not very good, and as a result, most of us came down with severe cases of dysentery. We started losing weight and soon became very weak. Even though we didn't have many things with us, item after item was slowly dropped along the way to lighten the load. I can remember one woman especially who had brought all she could carry. Day after day she left things behind so that when we arrived at the border she had almost nothing. Some of the territory that we passed through was not occupied by the Japanese and there we could sometimes travel by oxcart, mule, or buffalo.

The last ten days of the trip the countryside changed and we trudged over the mountains. All of us had sore hands and feet by now and our aching bodies were bleeding from scratches and open wounds. Our faces were burned by the rays of the sun and the clothes we wore hung loosely, in rags—yet we had to go on. If we stopped, the rest of the party would leave us to die. That was

13

the agreement we made and had kept from the beginning of the trip. In wartime China, you see, life was cheap.

Every night, even though I knew very little about the Living God and did not know Him in a personal way, I would cry out to Him. It seemed to me that I was the only one who thought anyone would help us but Buddha. Yet I wondered too at times if this God of mine would get us to freedom.

Two days before we reached the border our trip almost came to an abrupt end. Weary, we stopped to rest in a little shack along the path that we were traveling. Inside two very small rooms we huddled gratefully, and fell sound asleep. Suddenly with a loud crash the doors were broken down. We opened our eyes—there stood ten Chinese bandits. "Give us your money!" they demanded. Looking around they collected whatever earrings, watches, and other jewelry that had escaped the eyes of the Japanese soldiers. Almost all we had was handed over to them, with the hope of saving our lives. Nothing could mean anything more to us now than life and freedom. We were only a few miles from the border.

Three of the bandits had been smoking opium and it was obvious by the look in their eyes that they were half-crazed for more. When two of the men came over to where the women were sleeping and looked us over, we were terrified. I guess we were so ragged and filthy that they decided we weren't worth it and walked out of the room. As soon as the bandits left, taking with them what was left of our earthly possessions, we all got up and quickly fled for our lives. We knew that the Japanese would soon be there, because the traitors would turn us in for money. We were so frightened that we cried and screamed as we ran. We were only ten miles from the border. Could we, would we make it?

By morning we had come to a clearing about a mile wide, and we could see that Japanese soldiers were guarding the border. Our spirits fell; we had come so far, and now our chances looked hopeless. We could never get by these guards, with their sharp eyes! Many of the group felt that death was a certainty, my parents especially. We had spent thirty-seven days of living hell walking and running, being thirsty and hungry—all for nothing, it seemed. Everyone began to get cleaned up—to wash their feet, faces, and hands and change their clothes—for they knew that in a few hours they would try to cross the border. They expected, then, to be killed. It was a frightening thing for me, an eleven-year-old, to witness, for I knew when my people begin to wash up like this they are certain that death is at hand. The Chinese are afraid to die with dirt on their bodies. They must be clean to be received by their god. We didn't have much water so it was shared from one to another, until the last one in line was almost washing in mire.

I thought, *This is the time to talk to my friend, the Living God.* Out of the twenty-seven people, I was the only one who thought of praying. My father claimed to be a Catholic, but I had never seen or heard him pray.

Everyone was writing to their relatives so if they didn't survive, relatives would know what should be done with their possessions they had

15

left behind. This was in effect their last will and testament. I don't know how they ever expected anyone to receive the letters, for there certainly was no way for them to be delivered.

As we sat there waiting for the time to come when we would cross the border and run the last mile, all I could think of was those people washing. Then my mother came and washed me for death too. After she finished I was left alone again. In those few quiet moments I prayed silently, *Living God, can You hear me? I hope so, for right now we really need the help of a real God. Please help us across the border and make it so the Japanese soldiers don't see us. Someday please help me to see and know you. Thank You. Amen.*

As the blackness of night settled on the clearing our guide came over and said to us, "Now is the time." We all got up. As quietly as we could, not saying a word and hardly daring to breathe, we started walking toward the border. Then we broke into a run. We would walk, run, walk, run. Finally we crawled the last stretch until we could see freedom just ahead. With all the strength that was left within us, we got up and charged toward the border. For some strange reason the Japanese never even saw us. I wondered, *Could this God have heard my prayer and blinded their eyes?*

Finally we were there—across the border to freedom! "Freedom!" we shouted. The land of freedom was just a barren desert, but how wonderful it was to fall on that dry parched ground. Together we started singing our national song. The tears streamed down everyone's cheeks; the escape had been so hard for us.

As a little girl of eleven I decided then that

16

freedom must be a very important thing for a person to have. We had come a long distance, and how far I had come! None of the things that were mine as a little princess with her Shirley Temple doll had ever given me the joy that I was experiencing now. Freedom is not what kind of food we eat, or how beautiful the clothes we wear are, or how many cars we have. Freedom is a spirit we have. Yes, freedom of speech, a smile, movement, just to do as you please without fear of being killed. It would be ours here in the Province of Szechuen, and we were happy and relaxed.

Then suddenly we realized there were high mountains still ahead of us. We hadn't reached our destination yet! Once again it meant we must go through hardship, hunger, freezing cold, and walking. As we climbed the mountains, we became very much aware of the cold. Soon there was snow and with it our constant fear of frostbite and freezing. But frostbitten hands, feet, and faces were still wonderful in comparison to being tortured by the Japanese. When we thought we couldn't go any further we spotted a truck, one that had been left behind by the Japanese. It was a strange truck; I had never seen one like it before. It didn't burn gasoline but used charcoal as its fuel to run the steam engine. Gasoline was so scarce that it was reserved only for the tanks. We gathered wood gratefully and soon we were on our way with wheels under us.

The winding road through the mountains was very narrow. We had to get out of the truck because the wheels were at times only inches from the edge of the cliffs, and we were afraid that we would plunge to our deaths. Many trucks and buses before us had fallen over and hundreds of people had already died. After all the pain and misery of the journey we didn't want it to end like that.

It was a miracle how God had preserved all twenty-seven of us. Not one person had died. However, as we were on the last part of our journey toward Chungking, something rather funny happened that made all of us laugh. As we were sitting on the very few belongings that we had left and were happily bouncing down the road, all of a sudden someone said, "Where is Sun Kit Foo?" He was nowhere to be found. Suddenly he came running up behind the truck yelling, "Wait for me! Wait for Me!" He had taken a nasty tumble on his head. He climbed aboard, not knowing at the time that the cut on his scalp would take ten stitches to close.

We arrived in Chungking after the New Year, and the city was very quiet. There for the first time in several years I saw my grandfather. I was so afraid of him; all these years I had heard so much about him, how wealthy he was and how all the people feared him. As I looked into his eyes I could understand why people felt this way. I thought they were the meanest eyes I had ever seen. When I finally got to know him I realized all of the stories were not true, and I found him to be very kind.

My cousins gave me clothes and my mother got a dress from her sister-in-law and my father got clothing from his father. I will never forget how wonderful that first bowl of rice tasted. There were soft white buns, not the black ones. The food was so good I hardly wanted to swallow. And the clear, fresh drinking water—how wonderful it tasted. I remember the first time I had had to drink the filthy dirty river water—I didn't think I could swallow. I had seen the human refuse floating down the river and I said to my mother, "We can't drink this, we will die." But strangely enough, we hadn't.

So many things were new to us. I could hardly believe how much I had changed from the spoiled brat of two years ago who had demanded and cried for what she wanted, to a young girl who was thankful for a clear glass of water. Yes, I had a rather unusual beginning.... Let me tell you about it.

Chapter Two
THE MONKEY

I was born an illegitimate child in Yee Wo Hospital in Peking. My real mother was a teenager in love with a handsome opera star. She came from a high, famous family, was well-educated and also very beautiful as I was told in later years. My real father was very much in love with her. But in China one must marry only within the class into which he is born, and my mother was more high-born than he. Despite his talent the lovers could not marry. They did not know what to do with their baby, so they just abandoned it in the hospital.

Miss Soo, a cousin of my soon-to-be adoptive

mother, was a doctor interning at the hospital there in Peking when I was abandoned. I was a cute little baby. And since everybody loves babies, all the doctors chipped in money to feed me. Their generosity kept me from being transferred to a state institution. They soon realized, however, that a baby couldn't be raised under the supervision of so many people, and they had to find the baby a family.

My adoptive mother and father, who I will call simply Mother and Father from now on, had been married for years and they did not have any children. It had been verified by many doctors that my mother couldn't bear children. All of her relatives knew about her childlessness, so Dr. Soo started a correspondence with her about the abandoned baby in the Yee Wo Hospital.

I was born in the year of the monkey, on the fourth of September, in the Chinese way of counting, early in the morning before sunrise. According to custom, all these things tell the baby's future. In the Chinese tradition there are twelve symbols, one for each year; the monkey is one of them. We also have the year of the cow, the pig, the ox, the mouse, the lion, the dog, and others. All of these signs run in a twelve-year cycle. I was born in the year of the monkey, the symbol *Monkey* meaning lively, clever, intellectual, and understanding. These signs are very important when a family is thinking about adopting a child, and the exact time and day of birth must be determined before legal proceedings. Every sign must be right when the child comes to the family or it is believed that the adopted child could bring them bad luck.

My adoptive parents studied my symbol to find out whether it was a good one. According to the hour I was born, they figured out that I would sometime be very famous, rich, and very outstanding, more like a boy than a girl. I would also have a soft heart, a straightforward personality, and would always help the poor. They could, they thought, tell all my character according to the time that I was born.

My mother carried a red paper with the information and details of my birth with her all the time in a small purse. The purse was black with a little opal on the side surrounded by many little diamonds. Also in this strange little purse were two baby pictures taken moments after my birth. One picture was of my nose and the other one was of my ears. To the Chinese, the shape of the baby's ears is very significant. If a child's ears are like a cauliflower or stick out, he is considered likely to squander away family money and, hence, is not welcome. My ears were good—they were flatter than a pancake. You see, the child's face was very important in China. My facial features and the shape of my nose were also significant.

My adoptive mother had married into a very famous family, the Sung family. Her father-in-law was the general manager of the Bank of China for over forty years, and was well-known. He was also a chief stockholder of the bank, which had branches in New York, Paris, London, and in most of the big cities all over the world. For such a big and rich family to adopt a child is a very consequential step. My mother's position in the family was considered a disgrace because she had not borne a child for the family of Sung.

Nora and her mother

The decision about my adoption was the responsibility of my prospective father. Since he had graduated from the Lyon University in France as a medical doctor, his mind was more open to Western thinking. So he decided I was acceptable for adoption into the family and to be given the name of Sung. It was a great honor for me, because in China the name is all important. Throughout the years this family name stays the same, but every generation in each family has its own middle name. My name is Sung Neng Yee and so my cousin's middle names are all Neng too, such as Sung Neng Song, Sung Neng Kung, and Sung Neng Yu. So any child with the name of Neng going to school will be recognized by the teacher as being from the same generation. The middle name, or generation name, is chosen by a wise ancestor. Often the middle name used was actually given by an ancestor, in many cases, a number of generations ago. When all the names selected are used, another wise man is chosen to give new names for the next generations.

The doctors at the hospital had hired a nanny to care for me, and I was six months old when the Sung family decided to adopt me. Because of the long time I had been with the nanny I was so attached to her that I wouldn't go to anyone else. When we left Peking my mother hired her to fly to Shanghai with me. At home with the Sung family my nanny couldn't get used to the Shanghai dialect—nobody could understand her, and she couldn't understand them. Finally the Sungs bought her a ticket and sent her back to Peking.

Before the Japanese invaded Shanghai my

parents owned one of the largest estates in China. My mother had come from a very rich family. Her father was one of China's wealthiest merchants and one of the leading traders of seafoods with Japan. Her surname was Yip. He also had two wives, a practice which was very common in those days. He was so rich that he gave the Hung Ying Library, one of Shanghai's largest, to the government.

According to old Chinese custom, wooden doors should be matched with wooden doors and bamboo door matched with bamboo doors. In other words, marriage between two families should come because of mutual financial and cultural standing. If not, the couple will be looked down on. Chinese young people seldom marry out of their class. So it was in the case of my father. He came from a very wealthy and well-known family and naturally would marry someone who also came from a similar background. When my mother married my father, she brought with her a huge dowry, according to the tradition. The dowry included furniture, clothes for many, many years, and servants not only for herself but also for her husband. For years to come he would not have to buy clothing for himself; his new bride brought all of his wardrobe with her. It was very unusual for the bride to give servants to the husband, normally she just brought to the marriage servants for her own use. But since she was so fabulously wealthy the dowry also included servants for her husband. A large sum of money and many jewels were also included. All of the several thousand items of the dowry were listed in a red book. Red is a sign of good luck to the Chinese for marriage or for birth.

How fortunate I was to be adopted by such a wonderful and rich family! I was well taken care of by mother. She brought me the most expensive clothes from Europe and America. I was always dressed like Shirley Temple and was given a Shirley Temple doll that was always dressed like me. That doll would later become very important in my life. Almost every week in the *China Post* I was pictured on the society page modeling one of my new American outfits.

I was flatfooted and always had to have special shoes made because I didn't have any arch. My father was a doctor, and he thought because I had flat feet I would have headaches. He couldn't see his darling girl suffer so there were always special shoes made to order.

I was spoiled and pampered just like a little princess in the Royal Palace. From the moment I came to this family as an adopted child, for not even one moment was I alone. As I was their only child, they lived in fear of my health, so they hired a governess to be with me constantly. Even in the evening there was always a maid watching me or a nurse hovering over me. Not for one second was I even allowed to play in the yard, walk with the dog, or do anything else alone. There was the governess, gardener, chauffeur, maid, nurse, or a private tutor following me wherever I went. Soon I became used to having a constant companion with me and I enjoyed it. My parents were hardly ever home. They were socialites, constantly going to or giving parties, enjoying the night life of Shanghai to the fullest. As a result I did not see them very often.

One day while I was playing I ran down the stairs. How I remember that beautiful home and especially that beautiful staircase! As always the governess was following me, but this time I wanted to be by myself so I fled from her. As I ran down the staircase, my little feet caught in the thick red carpet and I fell. When she picked me up, I had a cut in the middle of my forehead.

Panic and fear took over all the servants. The princess had a cut—what would they do? The cook took some fish bone meal and rubbed it into the wound to stop the bleeding. Later when my father returned home he took me at once to the hospital; however, it was too late to properly cleanse the wound and I have the scar to this day.

My father scolded everyone on the household staff from the chief maid down to the chauffeur. Everyone was frightened because I was hurt—the dear little princess was hurt.

Whenever I wanted something I got it. My mother always said if the moon were not so high she would get it for me, if I wanted it. However, I was sentimental and often satisfied with simple things. Once my maid threw away my cloth toy dog. I cried and screamed, "You make a new one right now or I won't go to sleep!" "Yes, dear," she replied. She began sewing a new dog that very moment as I had demanded. I held my new dog and went sound asleep.

I always got what I wanted one way or another.

Chapter Three
MY LOST CHILDHOOD

When I was only a child of seven, the Japanese began bombing the wealthy districts in Shanghai. We were forced to leave our beautiful estate and flee for our lives. Overnight we became poor and dependent on others. My parents had owned many blocks of American stock. The Chinese market crashed and all this stock became worthless. Panic hit the city. Many formerly rich men couldn't adjust to loss, and there were suicides all over the city. My father, however, thought there were many ways to overcome his losses.

When the Japanese came the Chinese national

dollars were forced out of circulation and the Japanese forbade their use. They gave a very short time to exchange the currency into Japanese yen. So most of the people who were fabulously wealthy, even those having millions of dollars in the bank, overnight became almost penniless.

Soon the soldiers came and took our rings, watches, diamonds—everything they could get their hands on of any value. Then they came and took over our homes, giving us a few hours to clear out or be killed. We soon realized how cheap life was to them. Often they killed for the fun of it. We were allowed to take only what we could carry in our hands.

Because we were now without money we had to move into my grandmother's house. My grandmother was my father's stepmother—not his real mother. My father had gone to school in France at the age of thirteen just to escape the cruelty of this woman. He had asthma and bronchitis all his life because she didn't give him enough warm clothing during the cold weather in the country when he was young.

Now here we were, the three of us, in her home. I fared no better with her than my father. Because I wasn't born into the family, she hated me in a very special way. Overnight my princess-like childhood came to a close. I became a prisoner, living in a jail with my grandmother, at the young age of eight.

My grandmother's home, owned by the Bank of China, was something to behold. When we moved into the house to live, one unit of it was a new building, and one wing was the old home, decades old. My grandmother and her two daughters and their children lived in the new unit. We three—my father, my mother, and myself—lived in the old, haunted-like wing. Most of the rooms were closed down. It was a huge wing, and there were dirt and cobwebs all over. It was just like a devil's house in appearance.

This wing was dark and deserted, a frightening place for a spoiled "princess" like me. The entire first floor was used for hanging and drying salted meat. It could be stored like this for over one year.

As I would pass by the meat, there sat one of my grandmother's Buddhas watching over her possessions so no one would dare to steal a scrap. Everyone believed that the Buddha would tell my grandmother who had stolen it. As I walked by the meat the smell was beyond description and the shadowy strips looked like devils waving back and forth, back and forth. Oh, I was so frightened! Why had this happened to me? I just could not understand my new life. And the Buddha eyes—I couldn't bear to look at them!

Our wing was three stories high. We lived on the second floor and were given only one room with a bath attached. There were many other rooms on the floor but they were all closed up—reserved for my father's half-brother should he come to stay.

My grandmother was from the hill country, a farmer's daughter before she married my grandfather who was also a very poor farm boy from Chekiang. As a result, she knew nothing about hygiene. She was old-fashioned and had bound feet. Her feet were only a little over four inches long.

She was a worshiper of Buddha. There were statues of Buddha everywhere. All her belongings were watched over by a Buddha. How I hated the glass eyes of those gods of stone and clay!

Every day she would ask the Buddhas to tell her if one of the many servants had stolen something. She was always accusing someone of stealing her things. She yelled at everyone, scolding them from morning to night.

She also had strange eating habits. She would always eat every dish clean. She believed if she did this, it meant she would be able to buy one more acre of land—Buddha told her so. She was very superstitious, always doing this or that to keep Buddha happy.

I wasn't used to this Buddha-centered way of life. I could feel evil all over this wicked house. Wherever I went there were Buddhas with smiling faces. There were large ones and small ones along with the goddess of mercy and other idols. It was a nightmare of fear for me. I was always upset, and yet I knew there was nothing that could be done about it.

We were forced to eat the food that they offered to their idols. They not only worshiped the idols, but they also worshiped their ancestors. On every ancestor's birthday and deathday we had to light incense. Many special dishes were cooked and offered at the shrines. Everyone would come and kneel down before the idols of the ancestor and then we would eat this special food. After I heard of the living God later in mission school, I refused to eat it.

Everything was terrifying to me—the environment, my grandmother, the Buddhas—just everything. The next few years I spent most of my time crying because I was so lonely and felt forsaken. There were only three people living in the whole, big, old wing. When we came to my grandmother's all but one of the maids had been discharged. The remaining one had been brought along to do housework but she didn't live in the same house that we did. She lived above the garage and was with me only a few hours during the day.

My parents still went out very often in the evening playing mahjong and having fun as they were still young. So I was alone, and forlorn; this was loneliness like I had never known.

Soon I was enrolled in a school that was called McTyier School in Shanghai, a Christian school. There I started my six years of primary school. For the first time in my life I started to hear about Jesus, called the Son of God, who was living in the world. *How could this be?* I thought.

We sang hymns and the missionary told us the stories of Jesus and His love for children. We were also told that He wanted to be our friend. *How wonderful*, I thought. I didn't know much, but I started to realize that there truly was a living God. So lots of times when I was lonely and frightened, especially in the evenings, I would pray to my new friend Jesus.

Almost every night I was left alone and my parents wouldn't come back until the wee hours of the morning. Lots of times the phone would ring out in the long dark hall. It would ring and ring until finally shaking and terrified, I would slowly tiptoe out to answer it, only to discover the caller had hung up. At night the wing was more frightening than ever. It was like a creepy ghost house full of devils and demons.

There was very little furniture in our room.

There was only a bed and dresser for my parents. I slept on a box and put a chair at the end of it to hold my legs and feet.

We had no kitchen so we had to eat with my grandmother, aunts, and cousins who lived with her. They were all mean to me. They were taught by my grandmother to mistreat and scold me at the dinner table. Many times there were guests or relatives invited to birthday parties or occasions like "Winter Solstice." We Chinese have many special occasions to celebrate in a year. During these special days it was the custom for the children to bow down before their ancestors to show their respect. My grandmother or another adult called them one by one, the oldest first to the youngest, to bow down. The thing that hurt me most was that they never called me. They just ignored me, they didn't want me to have anything to do with their ancestry. I would run off and cry. I just couldn't understand why they didn't like me.

Everyone ate at a large table. Since my parents were usually away for dinner, I was the only one from my family eating with them. Again I was abused. The others always took the best pieces of food from the table and would let me eat only the leftovers and scraps.

The most difficult thing that I will always remember was that I was forced to eat and swallow the skin off of the duck's neck. My grandmother would say to me in front of everyone, "If you don't eat it I will have Buddha stab you with his chopsticks or pull your hair out." So in fear I swallowed the skin. Everytime I swallowed it tears came down my cheeks and I gagged. Many times I couldn't stop the retching and would run from the table to my room, with all of them laughing behind me. There was no food in our room so most of the time I was hungry. I didn't share these problems with my parents because I didn't want to hurt their feelings and worry them.

I was forced to grow up and I thought I must be brave. So I cried alone and continued to wonder why everyone mistreated me. I didn't know at that time that I was an adopted child. As my cousins yelled and taunted me, sometimes they called me a "wild seed from hell." I could not understand why, but it hurt terribly. At first I only heard this in the home. During the day I went to school and I felt better when I was with the other children. Then my cousins told some of my girl friends in school that I was evil and an illegitimate child. The rumors spread and my friends started to call me names and insult me. Then even school became a lonely nightmare. The maid would come after school to pick me up and soon she was calling me the "wild seed from hell" too.

One day I was so upset that I found enough courage to talk to my mother. My father wasn't home at the time. I said to my mother, "People call me dirty names and say I wasn't born by you. Would you please tell me the truth? I will then never ask you the question again."

"My child," she said, "sit down. It is true that I am not your real mother. You were born in a hospital and left there by your real mother who was from a rich family and very cultured. She was forbidden by her parents to marry your actor father who was out of her class. He was well-educated and very handsome but that didn't make any difference. So your father and I took you as our very own to love."

I looked at my mother with tears streaming down my cheeks and said, "Mom, I will behave the rest of my life and become a nice person, so that other people will respect you and me." Now, as never before, I became an adult. I didn't blame the people any longer for the way they treated me. Yet I was filled with self-pity. *Why do these things happen to me, just me?* I wondered. *Why did my real mom and dad have to abandon me?* I was so lonely that I started to talk to myself.

Then the Old Man came.

Chapter Four
THE OLD MAN

I got out of school at 3 P.M., and then there was only time—minutes and hours of time, of fear, and the horrible room. How I dreaded the long afternoon before going to bed and then, most of the time I was not able to go to sleep, but lay there listening to the shooting and screaming in the street.

I saw the Japanese soldiers do terrible things. People were hung right in front of everyone in the trees along the streets. The bodies would be left hanging until they decayed as a sign of the soldiers' power. The grim reminder worked! The people lived in fear and were afraid of the soldiers with their deadly bayonets.

As yet I did not know Jesus as my personal Savior. But every afternoon I would run from school, climb up the staircase to that room and cry aloud, "God, help me!" How I would pray to this wonderful God. I knew that the stone Buddha never helped. *Maybe, just maybe, this Living God could and would help*, I thought. I would talk to my Shirley Temple doll and tell her how this new God would help us. This doll was my only possession from my old days as "a princess."

One afternoon as I was waiting for the long hours to pass by, I felt a presence in the room with me. I was not at all frightened. I turned slowly toward the door and saw an old Chinese man standing there smiling. He spoke softly in Mandarin, a Chinese dialect. "Don't be afraid, I come from God," he said as he pointed toward heaven.

I noticed how very old he looked, older than anyone I had ever seen. He was wearing the clothing of a servant, a long, one-piece overshirt. *Where does he work?* I wondered. *Maybe he is one of Grandmother's new servants. He certainly doesn't look like a rich man.* He was very short with an aged, lined face, long white hair, and a very long white beard. As I looked at him I saw the kindest face I have ever seen in my life. In his eyes I saw love, a love that was what I had been asking this new God for.

The old man spoke again. "You don't need to cry because you weren't invited to your cousins' party." Although I had more beautiful dresses than my cousins, I wasn't invited.

I turned to the old man and cried, "I am so lonely—all the company I have is Shirley."

He slowly turned to me and said, "Nora, you have prayed, and I was sent by God to comfort and help you. Whatever things you want, I will get them for you."

I grabbed my doll, held her close to me and cried out, "Shirley, Shirley, did you hear that? The new God lives and He heard my prayer. We have a new friend, Shirley, do you hear? A new friend and he has been sent by God." I was so very happy because I had someone to talk to and I wouldn't be lonely anymore.

Suddenly panic hit me—I was frightened that he would go away and never come again to visit me. When he asked me what else I wanted, I added, "Promise me that you will come to see me whenever I ask." He promised. I didn't ask for chocolate, fancy food, or movies. All I wanted was someone to talk to me and be my friend; I wanted love. I was just dying for somebody to love me.

While we were talking I told him of my past, my adoption, and the way the family treated me. "Sir," I said, "I just can't go on living this kind of life. I would rather be dead than be this lonely."

"Someday Jesus will take away your loneliness," he said softly.

He kept his promise! He came back to visit me many times. I didn't even know how he got into the house or how he went out. I never paid much attention to these matters. I didn't know if he was really an angel or just an old man who cared for me.

The next day when I saw my mother I told her all about my visitor. She was amazed and asked me to call him to the room right then.

"Mother, he is my friend and he won't come while you are here," I said. He was a friend of Shirley and me—ours alone.

All this time we didn't have enough food or money. The Japanese took over all the food in Shanghai and they would sell rice only at certain times during the day. We had to line up to get our small amount of rice. You had to be there just at the right time or you wouldn't get your quota. Sometimes they would only give out the rice for one hour during the day. If a family had only one person to stand in the line they really had problems. Everyone rushed for a place in the line, shoving, pushing, screaming, doing almost anything for their bag of rice. It was always terrible, but starving people do strange things.

As a little girl I would take the responsibility of lining up for my parents. When I was near the front of the line they would come and buy the rice.

The soldiers would make a game of the line. They would take a switch to us and laugh. We dared not run or we would starve to death or be shot as we ran like frightened animals.

The old man came to see me almost every afternoon and would tell me when was the best time for me to go stand in the lines for the food and when there was danger and I was to stay home. He never misguided me. He was always right.

Mom was thrilled with my friend. She knew that he was really helping us. Soon she started to become dependent upon him and would ask me to call the old man for his advice or to do something for us.

My grandmother was mean to us so much of the time, and it was difficult for us to get enough food. To survive, my father decided we would quit eating with the others and would eat in our own room. So now we started to cook in the bathroom, and life became even more lonely.

I was always crying because the world outside was so big and it seemed out of reach for me. Here I was living in a big house with beautiful gardens, trees, flowers—but for me there was only the loneliness of our little room. The rest of the world was forbidden.

My cousins found another way to torment me. I could never get them to open the door for me when I came home from school. I was afraid the Japanese soldiers in the street would steal me or rape me or cut me up or do some other horrible thing. I would pound on the front door until my fists were red, screaming, "Mother, Mother, let me in! Please, won't someone let me in?"

I would see my cousins or grandmother look through the door glass and laugh and make faces at me. Then I would run to the back door and repeat the pounding and screaming. Then my cousins would yell, "Come to the front door and we will let you in." Sometimes this would go on for hours, while I ran from front to back. I thought I would go crazy with fear. No one ever stopped them from doing this.

I must be a big brave girl, I thought. *After all, I have my God friend.*

One afternoon the Japanese came into the school and took away the teachers who were missionaries. All the foreigners in Shanghai were interned together in camps, a fate for them almost worse than death.

I was worried that the old man would be killed by soldiers. I often wondered if my friend was a rickshaw man. Sometimes while walking home from school I would see the soldiers use a whip on the poor rickshaw men. They would just whip a man on his back until they beat him into the dust. If the man dared cry out, instead of the whip the bayonet might be shoved through his back and another man called to take his place. Life was so cheap.

As a little girl I had so much heartache both at school and at home. I was so lonely and miserable. My father was earning very little money, although he worked as a medical doctor for the Bank of China. We never seemed to have enough to eat, but I only wanted love and friendship from the old man and never asked him for food. How grateful I was to God that the old man kept coming back to visit me. He was my only comfort.

Sometimes I would come home so lonely that I would go into the bathroom and hug my mother's robe as it hung there and then pretend she was there with me. I didn't want to call the old man too much. I was afraid that he would get tired of me.

One day when he came to see me, he was very happy. He said, "I have good news for you, Nora. You are going to escape from Shanghai and this house of Buddhas. You will have a long trip and go to a faraway place and meet your grandfather." He was in Chungking and had been there since the war had started, not being able to return home.

I was so happy to hear this that I cried and laughed at the same time. I hugged the old man and together we thanked God for what He was going to do.

The first chance that came I told my mother and father what the old man had said. They could not believe it. My father asked, "Nora, when? How? Just exactly what did he tell you?" They wanted to believe it, for my grandfather was in Chungking. To go there would mean freedom. Chungking was the wartime capital of China. China is a very large country and never was completely occupied by the Japanese.

"Call the man back and ask him the question we are asking you, Nora, please," my mother begged.

"You both had better get out of the house so I can ask him," I said. "He won't come if you are here." They were very happy to leave this time. When I prayed and asked God to send the old man to come and see me, he did.

"Please, my friend," I asked, "my mother and father want to know exactly how and when we are going."

The old man answered, "It will be in about one week and you will go to the capital—Chungking." And as quickly as he came he was gone. Little did I know then it would be almost thirty years before I saw my friend again.

We had never had very much of a relationship with our grandfather. As a result we never heard from him or even received correspondence from him. So a week later when a knock was heard on the front door we were amazed. There stood a secret agent from Chungking on behalf of my grandfather, asking to speak to my father. The message he brought was startling. "Your father has sent me to tell your family to go at once to Chungking!" the agent said.

I remembered joyfully that this was the exact day when the old man said we would hear from the messenger God would send. Again this new God showed me He was alive and loved me.

It was a big decision for our family to make because this trip could easily result in our deaths. We were prepared to take the chance. I was glad because I was going to leave the loneliness of that room. I was not afraid. After all I was a big girl of eleven and the old man had said that we would get to Chungking alive.

The secret agent said to us, "The trip will be about 1,500 miles long. There will be no certain means of transportation to Chungking. You will have to walk much of the way crossing through the forest and climbing the mountains because you will be constantly hiding from the eyes of the Japanese soldiers. Before you can even think of crossing the border you will have many days and weeks to journey. Perhaps some of you will even die. Also, you must leave behind most of your possessions. You must go as beggars."

I packed my clothes and got ready to go. I picked up my doll and said to her, "Shirley, it will be hard but we will make it. God told me so."

Just then the agent said to me, "Nora, I am sorry but you will have to leave your doll behind.

A beggar child just would not have such a doll."

In tears I gave her to one of my cousins to keep for me until I could come back for her. How I loved that doll. Saying good-bye to Shirley was one of the saddest farewells I have ever had. "Shirley, don't be lonely, some day I will come back for you."

We had to look like beggars, with dirt on our faces and poor clothes on our backs. This was a new experience in fashions for me. "Mother," I cried, "do I really have to wear these rags?"

"Of course, so people will not guess that we are escaping to Chungking."

I realized she was right. Loss of pride, after all, was a small price to pay for freedom from the Japanese.

Chapter Five
CHUNGKING

There were many things that I really liked about being in Chungking.

My grandfather, Sung Han Cheng, was the general manager of the Bank of China and a very rich man. He had a private chef who cooked especially for him. Each day he lunched in the "Chief of Staff" dining room at the bank's headquarters. As his granddaughter I would sometimes go there to dine with him.

Chungking certainly was not as modern a city as Shanghai was, but even so, it meant freedom to us. In Chungking we didn't have any tap water in the house and, as a result, the bathroom facilities were outside. All the water we used we had to carry or buy, and that was very expensive. I soon learned again the value of fresh pure water. We were very careful about throwing away any water. We used it over and over in many different ways.

Taking a bath there was a delightful experience for me. I would drag a large wooden tub into the kitchen and then sit in it like a Buddha and wash myself. I would be about halfway through my bath when the tub would start to leak. I would have to hurry before the water ran all over the house. It never failed that when I would get the soap all over me, out the water would go. I would laugh and laugh at that silly old tub.

My father was given a job working as the bank doctor. When he started he didn't have enough clothes. He only had three shirts and he would use two a day. One he would carry with him because it was always so very hot in summer and he would need to change. I had to wash them right after he would come home. Of course, this had to be done on a washboard. Another hardship was that we didn't have any electricity, so I had to use a charcoal iron. The iron was so heavy I could hardly lift it, and it was a very dirty thing to use. I had to put the coal in and then try to get it to glow so the iron would heat up.

After a short time we learned how to use all of these things without electricity. The worst thing to cope with day after day was the water. We had to carry it from the river and it was always full of mud. We had to put alum in it so the mud would sink to the bottom and enable us to take the clear water off the top. Most of the people washed their bodies and clothes in the river, and we had to drink the same water.

The day we moved out of my grandfather's house into our own little home was a happy one for me and the family. That was the first time in many years we had a place to call our own. Soon after we moved into our home my parents sent me to a Christian boarding school run by American missionaries. It was here that I really learned a lot about the Son of God, who was already my friend. This school gave me the opportunity to know the Lord in a personal way, but I never made a commitment while I was there.

The school was so much fun. We did lots of singing and learned how to pray, especially before meals. This was easy for me to do because I really was thankful for the food. The devotions in the evening made me think how wonderful God was. We would pray for those that we had left behind and for our country that was torn by war.

In Chungking they spoke a different dialect than we did in Shanghai, so I almost had to learn a new langauge. Everything was all so new to me. The songs, prayers, and studies were a real challenge. I constantly reminded myself of my promise to my mother, *Mother, someday you will be proud of me.*

"I would like to be your friend if you want me to."

"Who said that?" I asked.

"I did," a girl replied, who was standing

behind me. And fast friends we became. Feng Yung Tat was a senior at the school and I was only in seventh grade, but she influenced my life greatly. Her father was a very famous Chinese man by the name of Feng Yuk Chung and is in our Chinese history books. He was a very famous general. The entire family were Christians and all loved the Lord very much. Every day she would tell me the wonderful stories about Jesus and would pray with me. How wonderful it was not to be lonely!

Feng Yung Tat had such peace and an outgoing personality and was always helping others. I admired her so much. Looking back now I would say that she influenced me to believe in Jesus more than anyone else in my life.

There were no streetlights in the outskirts of Chungking, and we had to carry torches when we walked home at night. Somewhere along the way we were always chased by a dog or two. The city was just full of dogs; they were everywhere. It was very rare that I could make it home without the torch burning out. Then the dogs really had fun, chasing us all the way home in the dark.

There were also bugs everywhere. At night they seemed to take over the entire city. Our beds were always full of them and every Saturday we had to take the mattresses outside and beat them. After a good beating the "bugs" came out, and we would try to kill them with boiling water. The people of Chungking cooked and ate right on the street and left the scraps there also. As a result there were bugs and more bugs.

Living in Chungking was like taking up residence in another country. The people dressed differently and even raised pigs in their homes. I remember the first time I saw all the men wearing white turbans around their heads, I thought they looked so funny and that they were having a funeral in their home. They believed they had to wear these or they would have headaches. There was a lot of bitter feeling between the two provinces, and now all of us streaming into Chungking didn't help the situation.

Soon we were to find out that the Japanese had not yet given up the hope of conquering all of China. They started bombing Chungking. The first time I heard the air-raid siren I thought all the demons of hell had been loosed. It was early one afternoon when I first heard the eerie wail of the horns. Feng Yung Tat grabbed my arm and said, "Run, Nora, the Japanese are coming with their airplanes to kill us!" And did we run! Several blocks behind the school there was a shelter, a cave in the side of the hill. We all hurried and crowded together hoping and praying that a bomb wouldn't fall close to us.

The nightmare of fear started all over again. One after another the bombs would scream as they sought a target. We could hear the cries of death and pain from those who did not make it to the hills. Later I would find out that those who had a quick death were the lucky ones.

Most of the caves had no water or food, and because of the large number of people crammed into them, many died of suffocation. I remember one time when the bombing did not stop for two and a half days. All this time we were without food, water, and proper sanitation. It was always so hot, and the stench was almost unendurable.

Sometimes a bomb would drop so close to the entrance to the cave that the ones near the front were killed. Many times I thought that one of these caves would become my tomb. It was not uncommon for a bomb to seal the front of the cave and all inside to be trapped within. Finally the all-clear siren would sound and we would return to our daily tasks as though nothing had happened. The bombings soon became a way of life.

In the summer of 1945 I was home with my parents for the summer break from school when the impossible happened. The news came on the radio at 4 P.M. and the papers carried the headlines: JAPAN SURRENDERS.

Chapter Six
THE RETURN TO SHANGHAI

Could the news really be true? I wondered. Knowing the power and hate of the Japanese soldiers I just couldn't believe that they would ever surrender to anyone. There was honor in death, and all of us believed that they would fight to the bitter end until every last one was dead. *It must just be some kind of trick*, I thought. I guess in reality none of us really thought that there was any hope for us winning the war.

My father came into the house crying with joy. "It's true. The edition of the papers is out and it's official. The Japanese have surrendered!"

We gathered around my father to hear the news. The stories were alarming, especially the one about the bombs that destroyed the cities of Hiroshima and Nagasaki in Japan. Almost everyone living in those cities was killed. It was terrible. But the atomic bomb had ended the war.

Everyone started to cry. Some were crying for joy because the hope of returning to their homes and loved ones could be a reality after eight long years of wartime separation. For some, however, their tears were of sorrow, because the war had brought eternal separation from members of their families.

All night long the city of Chungking was aglow with the flame of fireworks. They were going off everywhere. No one could sleep or even tried to; the excitement was so wonderful.

In the midst of all the noise I slipped off to be alone. I knew that I had to thank the wonderful God for the end of the war. *God,* I asked, *please help me to return to my city of Shanghai and some way, somehow, help me to really get to know You.*

Everyone was anxious to return to Shanghai. The government issued new money called the *yuan.* The quicker you bought things the cheaper they were, for inflation was soon to become a way of life.

I was anxious to get back to Shanghai and to go to school there. My mother and father promised that I could go to a school called the Mary Farnham School, run by the Presbyterians.

I hurried to the airport, only to discover that no seats on any plane would be available for months. My mother remembered that she knew

Passport photo

Nora as a young bride

someone in the military, and in a few weeks I was able to get a ticket on a military plane going to Nanking. What a thrill to look out of the plane window and think that I was returning to freedom and the chance to study in one of the best schools in China. The trip took just a few hours and I couldn't help but think, as we flew over the mountains, of the bleeding, hunger, and misery that we had all suffered just a few years ago. *But that is in the past*, I thought. *I have a wonderful life ahead of me.*

Soon the plane landed in Nanking and I caught the train to Shanghai. I was met at the train station by my mother's sister. As we drove to her home we passed the home of my grandmother. The cold chills ran down my back as I remembered those awful, lonely nights in the house. I wondered if all those Buddhas were still there guarding the hanging meat.

A week later I was enrolled in the Mary Farnham School. It was a boarding school so I lived in the dormitory. The school was really two schools in one. On one side of the campus was the girls' school and on the other was the boys' school, but they were off bounds to each other except on very special occasions.

The school rated very high academically and soon I found it very difficult to keep up with the other girls my age. Everyday I would hear remarks about knowing God as your personal Savior. *What do they mean?* I wondered. *That is just what I want, to know God in a personal way.*

The newly found peace that we were all enjoying was soon to end. We soon started hearing talk about a movement called Communism. At first all of us thought this would be a wonderful thing for China. But then we heard things that made us think of the beginning of the Japanese occupation.

The longing to know God in a personal way and the fear of prison turned my thoughts constantly to God. How thankful I was for the friends that I had made in the school. I would go with them to the chapel at school. It was open twenty-four hours a day. We would go there and talk about Jesus and the Bible and then we would pray. I loved to hear the girls pray. When they talked to God it was as though He was right there in the room with us. I longed to be able to know Him so that I could just talk to Him anytime in a real way and know, like my friends, that He heard every prayer. They knew He was a living God and their Savior.

The months passed and God still seemed far away from me. How my heart longed to know Him. During my freshman year in school, just before exam time, a notice was posted on the bulletin board that an evangelist would be speaking at the boys' school and the girls were permitted to attend. His name was Pastor Tong. Even though I was not sure about giving up the time from my studies, I decided I would go to the school matron and get my pass to attend the meeting. None of my friends were going to attend because of the final the next day. I was so hungry in my spirit to know Jesus that something compelled me to attend. I knew that getting an education wasn't the answer to all my needs. I really didn't know exactly what I was seeking, but I knew that I could find it at that meeting.

The girls were so concerned about the exams that many of them were asking their parents to bring them a flashlight, so they could study under the blankets after "lights out." I wondered for a moment if maybe I was doing the right thing by going to the meeting. *Maybe I should call my mother and have her bring me a flashlight, too,* I thought. I said to myself, *Well, I am not going to stay home and study during the meeting. If I find God He will provide for me. . . . Yes, I am going to hear what the man from the United States has to say about God.*

I left my room and went across the street to the boys' school. As I crossed the street I was amazed that I really wasn't worried about the test the next day. I didn't have a flashlight or any candles ready to study by, so I decided to enjoy myself.

As I entered the auditorium and heard the singing, I stood in awe and wonder. I knew somehow I would find Him. I knew that God was there to be found. In my heart I cried to God. *Please, God, I know that You are here, please let me find You.*

Soon I was sitting on the edge of my seat as I heard the man say, "Casting all your anxiety upon him..." (1 Peter 5:7) and then, "For God so loved the world, that He gave His only begotten Son, that whoever believes in Him, should not perish, but have eternal life." (John 3:16) Those words of God burned into my soul and I realized that God truly did send Jesus to earth to bring me, Nora, to Him.

When the evangelist said, "If anyone here tonight would like to find Jesus as their personal Savior and accept Him into their heart, please, while the music is playing, come forward." He didn't have to say it twice. This is what I had been praying for all these years.

With tears streaming down my cheeks and my body shaking like a leaf in a storm I rushed forward, knowing that I would be forgiven by God and become His child. Yes, I was going to find Jesus. As I prayed and asked Him into my heart as my personal Savior I immediately felt the emptiness and the worries leave me. I was floating on air with the joy of the New Birth. He was mine. I was now the daughter of God, the child of the King.

On my way back to the dorm, I was singing, laughing, crying. Oh, the joy that was in my heart! When I saw the school janitor holding a flashlight in his hand I didn't hesitate for a moment to ask him to loan it to me. I ran to him and asked, "Could I please use your flashlight tonight to study?"

He didn't ask me for my name, what grade I was in, or anything. He just looked at me and said, "Yes, you can use it," and then handed it to me.

The Lord had already provided for me—I knew for sure that I was His child. There was no way to get a flashlight except by a miracle of God, and everyone was trying to borrow or buy one. As I was lying under my blanket studying I knew God was by my side. How wonderful!

All night long I read and crammed for the test hoping and praying that God would help me to remember all the things that I had worked so hard all year to learn. He did. The next day I passed all my tests and entered my junior year of high school.

A few weeks later I decided to proclaim my new faith in Christ by following His command to be baptized. This was an important decision, for then all would know that I had become a Christian. I didn't care what happened. If Jesus Christ could come to the earth and die for me, then I was willing to do the same for Him. So I was baptized. Little did I know then that my faith would soon be put to the test.

Chapter Seven
THE FALL OF CHINA

Being an only child and a girl in China is nothing to feel proud of. The desire of every family is to have a son who will carry on the family name. Of course, that was the constant burden of my father; he had no son.

My father's brother was a soldier in the United States Army. He held the rank of Captain and served as a dentist. In Army tradition, he was always being transferred and the war had brought him and his family to China. Their son was two years old. On one of these transfers this child had the measles. Since he could not be moved from one city to another, they left him in the care of my mother and father. Soon after they moved to Peking my aunt gave birth to another son. Weeks turned into months and still the boy stayed with our family. Then another child came along and then another.

One day my aunt wrote and told my mother, "You may keep my boy and make him your very own son. We have enough children!"

Perhaps this sounds cold, but abandoning him to us was really an act of love, for my aunt was very concerned that there was no son in my father's household. There were no legal papers; the son was just a gift. It is very common in China when one brother has two or more sons and his brother has none that there is a gift of a son. It is a Chinese custom that when a father dies the son carries the head of the coffin and the daughter carries the foot. So my new brother brought much happiness to our family.

Happiness? I soon learned that the only means of happiness is to live and serve the Lord Jesus. Peace? There is only one real peace, and that is the peace of spirit that the Lord Jesus gives to His children.

The years have passed since then. Today my brother is behind the Bamboo Curtain. How our hearts grieve for him. My mother prays daily for his release and safety. The last information we had is that he works for the Bank of China. His pay is very low.

In just a few short years after the end of the war there were dark clouds of fear casting their shadows again over my country. The thought of leaving Shanghai again was more than we could bear. But the sound of the guns soon made us realize that our days of safety were numbered. Everyday the communists were getting closer and closer to the city of Nanking and the eventual overthrow of the government.

None of us really knew just what the Communists stood for or just what would happen when and if they did take over the government. Some rumored that they would force the girls to marry men chosen for them. Others said they would not allow us to keep our possessions, and the rumors continued until no one knew what to believe.

Rather than take a chance, many of the families started to leave the country. Some went to the United States, others fled to Hong Kong, and most went to Taiwan. The poor had no choice but to remain and face whatever fate was theirs. Even many people of means because of various circumstances were forced to stay.

My father said, "Well, we just don't have any place to go. We were raised in China, and we don't have any friends or relatives in Hong Kong or the United States who have offered to help. We will have to stay here and see what happens to us."

Soon my mother's sister and her husband decided that they would go to Taipei, Taiwan with their children and begin life anew. I was very close to her so I asked if I could go with them. Mother said, "I will not leave your father alone but, Nora, if you want to go you may."

I knew that she was hurt to think that I could leave the family so I quickly replied, "Mom, you don't want me to marry a Communist, do you?" The next day I boarded a freighter bound for Taipei. It took me three days to reach the island.

When I arrived there I was shocked. In those days there was hardly anything new—everything was old and dirty. My aunt's "apartment" was two rooms above an office with no water or modern toilet facilities. To make things even worse, it was winter and there was no heat; all night long we would lie there and almost freeze to death. In the small bedroom there was no thought of the luxury of a mattress, let alone a bed to put it on. There we were huddled on the cold floor, shivering the whole night long on the top of a quilt.

I rationalized that Communism couldn't be so bad. I missed my mother and father, so I thought it would be better to die with my parents than to stay here in Taiwan. Before long I caught another freighter home to join my parents. I arrived back in the mainland just after the new year.

The short months of spring brought continuous word of communist activity. By summer they had control of China, and the government of Chiang Kai-shek was forced to leave the mainland.

I remember the night that my country fell into the hands of the Communists as though it were only moments ago. We lived very close to the police station and could hear the steady staccato of machine guns pelleting their bullets out all night—and then the eerie silence. The next thing we heard was that the police were marched out of the building with their hands behind their heads and the Communist soldiers marched in, taking over authority from the police. Then we heard that they had taken over the radio station and the airport, so now there was no way of escape. There was no transportation except that controlled by the Communists. Everything stopped that day—everything. We all knew then that the Communists were in power. None of us realized the cruelty of the Communists, so we were looking forward to the news of what had happened to get a better idea of Communism. Most of us, to be quite frank, were blinded by their propaganda. Leaflets and newspapers and magazines heralded a new age, the new freedom of Communism. At the time of the takeover I was in my second year of high school, and right away things became very confused. The Communists put a teacher in from the People's University in Peking and soon our books and literature became communistic.

During those first years in Shanghai there wasn't much change, but we had heard by the grapevine that there were terrible things going on in the country. We heard that many landlords had been shot and some people in key places were killed. Little did we know then that the Communists had killed twenty-five million Chinese. In those first years the American movies still played, the dance halls were still open—just like the old days. But gradually the movies were closed, or at least all the American movies were stopped, and soon all the movies to be seen were only those permitted by the Communists. After that there was a complete takeover of the schools. Anyone who was old or from the old way of life had to go and was replaced by the new young people of Communism. However, even the Communists realized that a doctor couldn't be trained overnight, so many of the old doctors were kept on for quite a while. My father was a doctor and was kept at work by the Communists. The first religious group to be prosecuted were the Roman Catholics. My father had this mark against him, as he had been taught in a Catholic school.

Then the day came when we were all to realize what the true meaning of atheistic communism really was. This nightmare began on the eve of the 1950 Chinese New Year. That morning the people greeted each other as always, one relative to another bowing to each other and wishing each a wonderful New Year. Later on that day the riots started. Many of the local people displayed the Communist flag in the streets celebrating this happy time in China.

Then some of the Communists from the hospital took my father away and put him in a hospital room. It was a very tall building and they put him on the top floor. We were told that no one could visit him and he couldn't return home either. They wanted him to confess and to write a life story. They interrogated him day and night, night and day trying to force him to reveal his association with this person or that friend, did he know this one or that one, what did this one think, what did that one think. . . . Cleverly they tried to plant deceit in his mind by saying others had accused him.

Oh, how clever they were in this thing called "brainwashing." They would sit him on a little stool in the middle of the room, with the glare of lights in his face, and then accuse him again and again of all sorts of things. They spat upon him, used dirty words to hurt him, resorted to anything—trying to get him to confess the things all of them knew he had not done.

This went on for two weeks. Then they repossessed the house where we lived as payment of our debt. They said the action was done because my father had stolen money from the hospital. They wanted him to confess to this, but he wouldn't. Finally when it was apparent he wasn't going to confess, they released him and told him that the hospital didn't need him anymore. We were ordered to move away.

Gathering together what few belongings we could, again we became refugees in our own land. We walked far out of town into the terrible slum factory district and there we found an old home that was quite junky. We were given a little room that was attached to the side of the building. All the walls were broken down, there was no paint, and the windows were broken out. It was just terrible but we had nowhere else to go, so we moved in. My mother, father, brother, and myself moved into that one little room. We were fortunate, however, for there were five other families in that home and each family had one little room of their own. We all used the same kitchen and in this little house there was no bath or toilet facilities. It was very difficult for us to face this kind of situation again.

Soon the Communists came and took my father away. This time it was not to interrogate him but to put him to work as a doctor in a clinic. There he was forced to treat a hundred patients each day and was given a little money on which we could live.

Soon we realized the terror of men who try

to block God out of existence. These people were heathen. They didn't believe in God and had set out to destroy Christians. Ministers and priests were either jailed or killed or punished. It was just terrible.

The effect the Communists had on the people was amazing. As I look back today, I see how close I was to being duped—brainwashed by them. I was teaching about Communist leaders in school at the time and I'd describe the Communists as heroes and tell how they had fought all these years to liberate China. As I read their material over and over again I almost believed that was true. Yes, I also had quit going to church; I didn't read my Bible; I didn't pray. God seemed to have been blotted out of my life.

In 1950 I was studying at law school. Most of the professors that were there when I started at the University were still there. Almost everyday we heard about a certain professor being gone, or another one shooting or hanging himself because he couldn't stand the torture. And other professors just disappeared. The school became an unacademic mess. The law school that I was attending was a Christian school, but soon all Christian activity was stopped and no one dared to mention the name of God or religion. I felt badly, even though I wasn't participating, that religious freedom wasn't allowed.

Today my heart cries out as I see in America day by day this religious freedom being taken from our schools. Oh, my friends, if you could only realize the subtle inroads of Communism!

Chapter Eight
SAVED FROM DEATH

In 1953 I graduated from the Soochow University Law School and soon earned my LLB degree in law, with honors. I was twenty-one years old, and because I had proved to be an excellent student I was accepted by the university as an assistant professor. There I was, a young girl with two pony tails, teaching in the ranks with some very important men of China. It wasn't long until I became proud of my accomplishments and of my own knowledge.

Pride is a destructive cancer. When a person becomes proud, I don't care how young or how old he is, or what kind of pride he has in his heart—spiritual, material, anything—as long as it is there, this pride is the beginning of the end. I thank God now that He didn't just cast me away, but He was really calling me back to Himself.

The punishment began in 1950. In our family the persecution started with my father and continued until he died. Then in 1955 the punishment included my husband and me. We weren't fully aware of what was going on because it was only mental.

Both my husband and I were graduates of the same law school. I can remember as though it were only yesterday the first time I saw him in the schoolyard. He was very tall and good looking. Later I learned that he played the piano well and that he was very quiet—seldom talking to anyone. It was rumored that he had strange idiosyncrasies and had never dated any girl. A group of girls in the university made a bet that none of us would be able to have a date with him. I was challenged; the will to win was my nature. I accepted the bet and told my girl friends that within two weeks I would have a date with this peculiar young man. One day I had two concert tickets and saw him among a group of classmates. I gathered my courage and went up to him and invited him to go with me to the concert. To my surprise he accepted. I was very glad that I had won the "bet." This was the beginning of our romance.

We dated for four years and then agreed to get married. We registered with the authorities so we could live together. In Red China there is no marriage ceremony in church.

The honeymoon was short-lived, and I knew that something was wrong. I kept all of our misfortunes to myself for I had to save face.

In 1955 I became a special instructor at a high school that wasn't actually a high school, but a school where we gave six years of instruction in three years of concentrated teaching. I wasn't teaching normal children, however. I had been selected with other teachers to teach the Communist war soldiers. Some were spies, and some secret agents, and in their own way, they were all very brilliant fighters for the Communists. But they lacked the essentials for being leaders in the country. They were not well versed in the history or the machinery of government. I was selected to teach these men political science and history. Oh, I was respected and, of course, useful to the Communists. I became very proud of myself and my accomplishments. As a matter of fact, for two years I basked in the glory of Communism. Church no longer was a part of my life. I wanted to have nothing to do with Christianity any more. During this time once I even denied the Lord. Their logic about evolution and the monkey becoming man and the fables of the Bible became so real to me that I could hardly believe in God. In essence, I became a heathen.

The glory of Communism swept across China and one couldn't help but get caught up in it. If you were involved there were benefits: pride, prestige, esteem, and ego satisfaction. I thought to myself many times, *That is just what I want to be—a Communist.* But then all of this dream came to an end, just like a bell ringing, and woke me up to the truth of Communism and the filth that was all about me.

It wasn't an abrupt, quick change. But it was something very subtle. I really can't remember when I first became aware of the deceit and deception of the Communists. The school I was teaching in was called Tung Tsi, a very famous architectural school before the Communists took it over. It included a high school and a university. Now here we were in the midst of it with almost five thousand people including teachers and students living behind the walls of the school. One of the first things I started to question was why the doors of this school were suddenly locked, not only to keep those on the outside out, but keeping us who were on the inside in. The Communists don't move about very much and I soon learned how their brainwashing was carried on. Night after night we would hear an ambulance come to pick up an old professor or one who could no longer stand the Communist torment. Suicide was their only way to freedom.

When I was pregnant with my first child I was bothered with morning sickness and as a result I seldom could eat breakfast. One of the school routines was a requirement that we go to the auditorium every morning. There we listened to the sayings of Mao Tse-tung and absorbed his wonderful ideas. Only then could we go to work. Everyday, day after day after day, Mao Tse-tung started our morning. Oh, what a lesson we Christians should glean from that—we should read our Bible and pray and then start our day. During the day there would be meetings and this teacher or that student would be named to lead the service or the meeting, as they would call it. They always planned ahead who would be put to "the test." The day came when they started looking at me. They said, "Nora, we want you to say something about this professor, anything you can remember, to show how he was against the Communists." Then another one said, "Nora, I don't understand about your mother. Why is she always with a missionary or a minister, and speaking English?" They had found out everything. Then another person said, "Nora, we've got to let you say how your grandfather became so rich. Why is he the big wheel in the Bank of China? Also, why did your father go to France to study at thirteen and return fourteen years later as a medical doctor?" Then another one asked, "Nora, do you know anything about Christianity? We heard once you were a Christian. Were you?" All these questions came at me day after day and I knew that my day to face them was coming.

At first, I thought maybe they are just kidding and it would be over soon. But I knew deep within my heart that this would continue endlessly. I soon found out that I could not go home to visit my parents anymore. I knew that I could not call upon my mother to help me. There was no one in the world who could help me. How well I remember that dark, dark night in my life.

My thoughts returned to the day I went forward and came to Christ and how I repented. I remembered how I had said to Him, "Lord, you know when a person comes to the end of the world it's the beginning of You. Lord, if this is the time you want me to come back to you, oh, please cleanse me of my sin and give me strength, give me strength to go all the way with you, Jesus, even if it means I must die for you. Please, please, Christ, forgive me!" I meant every word of that prayer and I knew that it was a great decision. As I asked for forgiveness, oh, what a great release came from Heaven and peace and joy came down. It's such a hard thing to describe this peace and joy. It's not how much money you have in the bank or how big your job is or how influential you are. It's just facing your enemy when you are about to die with an overwhelming flood of joy.

"Now," I said, "Lord, I have not served you for so many years. I don't go to church and I haven't read your Word. But could you please help me?" And then once again the Lord released His Holy Spirit and gave me grace and mercy. The Spirit of the Lord spoke to me and said, *Nora, you don't need to worry about what kind of word you're going to speak. I am going to speak through you. You don't need to worry. They can only kill your body. I am with you and no one can be against you.* God performed a miracle and flooded my mind with a multitude of verses from the Bible. I hardly even knew these Scriptures at that time. With this encouragement I started my stand like a real Christian soldier.

In the afternoon they started hounding me with all kinds of questions such as: "Is your mother a Christian? Is your father a Catholic?" They continued along this line of why this, why that? Do you know that person? Why did you have lunch with this one? Why were you talking with that one? Then the crucial question was repeated: "Nora, are you a Christian?" I paused for a moment, knowing full well that after the way the Spirit of God had spoken to me there was only one answer that I could give. I looked straight into the eyes of my persecutors and said, "I have not been acting like a Christian but I am one and I am proud of it. Do whatever you want to with me, but just don't kick me around, please; I'm pregnant." They didn't care whether or not I was pregnant and they said, "From this moment on we just won't feed you any more."

I started to talk to my son even before he came into the world as somehow I knew he would be a boy. *My son, my son, you've got to obey your mother. We are both passing a great trial now. I don't have any food to feed you. I don't know how long it will be—water or food—but you have got to fight with your mother. Even though you haven't come into this sinful world you must fight with me.* And I prayed. Oh, how I prayed. The morning sickness left me. I didn't vomit as I used to. The strangest sensation came over me and I didn't feel hungry from that morning until the very next day. All this time the interrogation was going on and on. They wanted me to write down everything I said. Whatever I answered they wrote down and then they put my fingerprints on each piece of paper to verify that what I said was true. *Why would they do this if they were not going to shoot me?* I thought. My interrogators were so tired that they finally walked out of the meeting. Then another group would come in and they would leave exhausted. Then another group would come in. There were more meetings and more feelers. The feeling of hatred from them was so strong that it was just like they wanted to eat me up. It was a strange thing but I still had the peace that the Spirit of God had placed in my heart.

Then the night came. They were so mad at my denials and refusals to lie that finally one screamed, "Take her out to the desert and shoot her!" The idea appealed to them, so I was ushered out into the dark. As we walked they kept saying, "Cry out! Confess! Confess!" But in my heart there was only joy. As we got a little way out into the desert I saw an armored car with a machine gun mounted on its top. Nearby there were seven soldiers with guns in their hands ready to fire. Then I was asked, "Do you have any last words to say? What would you like? What would you want for the last moment that you're alive?" Then they told me that if I would talk they could help me. I knew that they were all liars. Also I knew that if I said anything they would just use it to persecute someone else. So I thought to myself, "I won't say a word to anybody." I merely looked at them and said, "I have nothing to say."

Someone blindfolded me and led me out to the stake. Then they gave me three minutes to think about it; I thought and I prayed. Oh, how hard it was for me to stand there realizing that there were only three minutes left for me on this earth. There were a lot of things I thought of, a lot of things I would like to have undone. I almost got to the place where I was numb to all feeling and thinking. I didn't even know how to pray or what to pray.

Then all of a sudden I seemed to have a stubborn thought and I said, *Lord, this just doesn't seem to be the time for me to die. I'm pregnant*

and my son, my son, he hasn't been born yet.
Lord, all these experiences, can't they glorify your
name somehow? But, Lord, if this is really the
time I should die, then I am ready to go. Forgive
me, cleanse me, and take me into your arms.

And while I was praying like this I didn't
realize what was going on but I felt a warmth
and a glow. The entire place was bathed in a
brilliant shining light from Heaven. They lifted
their guns and pulled the triggers and the bullets
came leaping toward me. I really don't know
whether they missed me, whether they went over
me, under me, or whether they were stopped in
midair, but not one bullet touched me.

They took me from the desert back to the
school. I was told by a girl in the rest room
that the whole place was blinded by a light from
Heaven and they didn't know why, but all the
soldiers were so afraid. I told the girl, "Oh, I'm
sure that was Jesus." This was the first sermon
I preached to my enemy.

Then they started to ask me how these things
could happen, and I told them that this supernatural manifestation was from God. My God is
a God who raises people from the dead and, of
course, if He could do that He is able to keep
them alive. God had kept me alive. What joy
was in my heart!

They were so exasperated with me that the
meeting went on all night and into the morning
hours. All this time I didn't have anything to
eat or drink. My whole body was swollen. The
discomfort was so hard to bear. I was taken back
to my room by four men because I couldn't walk.
They almost dragged me the whole way. They

put me on a bed and I slept like a baby the rest of the day. I didn't even know that the four were watching me the entire time. They were afraid I might disappear and they would be deprived of another victim to torture.

During the night a dream came to me while I continued to sleep like a baby. In the dream the Lord gave me Psalm 18 from verse 1 to 6.

I LOVE Thee, O LORD, my strength.
The LORD is my rock and my fortress and
   my deliverer,
My God, my rock, in whom I take refuge;
My shield and the horn of my salvation, my
   stronghold.
I call upon the LORD, who is worthy to be
   praised,
And I am saved from my enemies.

The cords of death encompassed me,
And the torrents of ungodliness terrified me.
The cords of Sheol surrounded me;
The snares of death confronted me.
In my distress I called upon the LORD,
And cried to my God for help;
He heard my voice out of His temple,
And my cry for help before Him came into
   His ears.

Well, I thought, *as long as the Lord heard my cry that's it. I don't need to worry about anything.* I had assurance that I was going to get out of Red China. I didn't know how, when, or where. But I knew that the Lord knew and that was all I needed. I had peace from that day on.

The persecution didn't stop in just one day. It continued for two years, which seemed like an eternity. They took away my job and I couldn't teach anymore. Immediately I became a marked person. Nobody talked to me. I became like a leper—a dead person walking among the living. When I sat at the table no one else would sit there. Some days they allowed me to go home and some they kept me in the school. I found out later that they kept my husband in the court where he was working and they kept my father at the hospital. So there we were, in three different places, and unable to communicate. They alternated breaks: one day they would let me go home, on a different day my father, and at another time, my husband. Hardly ever did all three of us arrive home at the same time. When it was time to say good-bye to my mother after my brief visit at home I would say, "Mom, I don't know if I will ever meet you on this earth again. But if this is my last day we will certainly meet in heaven."

Every single moment during these days we lived in fear and doubt. This was very hard for us because we never even thought about material things any more. We didn't care what we were going to eat or how we slept or anything else. The mental torture was so severe that all we could do was pray and cry out to the Lord through the tears, trusting that somehow, someday there would be deliverance from the hands of the enemy. Again I realized the importance of freedom and how far from my grasp it seemed to be. Yet I knew that God would provide a way of escape.

Nora as a University Student

Chapter Nine
BEGINNING OF FREEDOM

It is strange how a woman who is expecting her first child can be so much more concerned about the life within her than her own. That was my case. As a matter of fact, I think that this pregnancy was the thing that kept me mentally alive. For even though the time was drawing near that I would deliver my child, the mental and physical torture did not let up.

Sometimes I would be dragged before a big meeting. There would be several hundred people there and everyone would crush around me to listen to my confession. They would kick me, slap me in the face, and do everything they could think of to insult me. Many times they would all leave me sitting alone in a room for several days, so I could experience the silent treatment where no one would talk to me. No food and no water would be provided—just loneliness and darkness. These were moments when Jesus was very precious to me. I would pray and feel His love bathe my body and I would not be afraid. I knew His presence; I was not alone, I would rest upon His promises of peace and joy and deliverance. Then they would come in again with papers and would want me to write my history, my childhood memories. They would read and reread them over and over trying to find something, so they could accuse me of something again. Then I would have to write it and rewrite it. They would also ask me to write about someone else with the idea of my incriminating a friend or contradicting myself. But God constantly guided my thoughts.

In the lonely hours I would talk to my baby telling him how much God loved him and was caring for us. In late January of 1956 I was thin and sick because of the lack of food. There were times when waves of depression would come upon me and I would think, *Oh, is my son all right or will he be a mental case? Can he possibly be all right after all this?* And I would worry that perhaps my fear and my fright and all this mental anguish that I was going through would be somehow transmitted to my son. I would cry out to the Lord not to allow this to happen. Then I would feel His peace again, through my tears.

On the eve of February 17 my labor pains

set in and I knew my child would soon be here. I was so weak that I didn't know what to do; I could hardly speak. I begged the nurses at the hospital to help me, but they just let me lay there. I thought I would bleed to death. There was no one to help—they didn't care. As a matter of fact, I suppose they were hoping that I would die. My child was born after seventy-two hours of labor, and they told me I had a son. The tears of joy and relief flooded down my cheeks when I heard he was healthy. At that moment, lying there alone in my bed, I gave him to God to be His servant. When finally I held my son in my arms I was thrilled to see that he had rosy cheeks and a strong body. Truly God was a God of miracles, for I delivered a healthy son.

After a week I was discharged from the hospital and was permitted to go home. Because this was my first son I didn't have any idea how to care for a child or even change a diaper. My mother was there and helped me. How thankful I was for my mother! The worst thing I recall now was that we didn't have any heat and it was so cold it was hard to change and bathe the baby. We couldn't wash him very often. About every two weeks we would gather some charcoal and make the room very warm and bathe him.

A few days after we arrived home from the hospital I was told I had to return to the school, that I shouldn't get any ideas that I had been released. After this I had to catch the bus every morning, rushing out after changing and feeding my baby to sit and be interrogated. Sometimes they would allow me to go home at night and sometimes I would be expected to stay there for several days. I was trying to breast feed my baby but in all this confusion my milk was soon gone. Then there was another burden of finding where to get milk to feed my son. I would take the few pennies I had and buy the milk. Then it was a matter of trying to find someone who would take the milk to my home by the bus. In the midst of all this day-by-day confusion God provided. Somehow, someway, we managed to survive.

The money from my school job was very little and we lived mostly on the money that was sent to us by my mother-in-law from Hong Kong. My husband was working in the courts at the time and he was also being punished by the Communists. Both of us were living in constant fear. It wasn't long, as a matter of fact only a few months, before I realized that I was expecting my second child. It was hard to bear the thought of bringing another child into this life of misery and trials.

Soon word came that my father was placed in a hospital for "observation and treatment" as the Communists called it. How my father had suffered under the piercing eyes of these people! He was the son of a very wealthy man, and the change was harder for him than the rest of us. My grandfather, of course, was a very wealthy man and his life and his deeds are recorded in the history books of China. He built a huge hospital called Young Ming, built many schools in his native province of Chekiang, and contributed to many other worthwhile causes. His family consisted of three sons and two daughters, and his accomplishments included the reading and writing of Spanish, French, and English.

Before the Communists took over Grandfather moved to Brazil and, of course, could not return. Because of all this my father had to suffer. His torment started in 1950. My father was a very honest man and tried to tell the Communists everything they wanted to know. As I have mentioned before, he was placed in the country where he was expected to treat over a hundred patients a day. Because of his weakened condition, he got the flu. At first they allowed us to visit him in the hospital, and I tried the best I could to care for him. I can remember many times going there and washing his feet, trying to bring the fever down. My father looked at me one day and said, "Oh, how I wish I could be out of here for just one day and have a one day holiday away from all this torment."

For the Communists there is no such thing as a holiday, not even on Saturday or Sunday. There is always something to do—always work to carry out. I said to my father, "Dad, even though we don't have a place to picnic and no car, we would certainly enjoy having you at home, just to sit around and talk."

So we started planning things to do the next day when he would be released from the hospital. My father looked very bad; he was so undernourished and he was coughing. But the fever was gone and I thought they would surely allow him to come home for a day. But it didn't happen. I asked them if I could stay at the hospital all night to be with him, thinking that I could help.

During the quiet, dark hours my father called me to his bed and said to me, "Nora, come here and listen closely to what I have to say. I want to share something with you."

"What do you want to share?" I answered. "You can tell me tomorrow. You'll be getting out of the hospital, won't you?"

He said, "Well, maybe. But, Nora, they are testing some new kind of medicine on me."

I said, "A new kind of medicine! Dad, why are they doing that? Why are they testing medicine on you, a doctor?"

His reply was, "I really don't know, but there was a trusted Communist doctor who came to see me this morning. He gave me the medicine, and he didn't know exactly what it was himself. But when I took it, after a few hours I started to bleed. Now I notice that I am bleeding quite severely from my bowels."

I cried out in dismay: "Nurse, come here! Come here! Why is it that my father is bleeding so? You must give him a blood transfusion. Otherwise it will be too late!"

"Oh, don't worry," they told me. "We know what's going on." But finally they did come in and give him a transfusion.

How he began to suffer! He was so thirsty. When a person bleeds he gets very thirsty. He begged and begged for water, but the doctor had ordered there was to be no water for him. If I had known then this would be the last day I'd see my father, I would let him drink as much water as he wanted to.

But I said to him, "Now, Dad, don't beg for water. You know the doctors said you couldn't have any. Don't act like a kid. You're a doctor. Why do you want water when the doctor told you you shouldn't have any?"

I didn't realize that this doctor was testing medicine from Russia. So I said, "Be good. I'm going home to sleep and mother is coming out to see you."

My father said, "Oh, Nora. Please give me some water. I'm so dry and thirsty. Please!"

At that time he was still getting the medicine which I thought they had already stopped giving him. They deceived him by telling him it was vitamins. My ride home on the bus and the train took me about an hour and a half. While I was on my way home, Mom was on her way to the hospital. When I left him the fever was gone and I thought, *My father will be all right.*

Mother arrived at the hospital and was stopped at the door; they did not allow her to go up to his room. "Call your family as quickly as possible," she was told. "Your husband is in very dangerous and critical condition." They didn't tell her that he was already dead.

When my mother called and gave me this news I left immediately on the train and bus to get back to the hospital. They still had not allowed her to see my father when my brother and I arrived. Then they brought us up together to see my father. A sheet had already been drawn over his face.

When they took away the sheet, we could hardly see him because the curtain and shade over the window had been drawn to darken the room. As I looked at him I could see that every opening of his body was seeping blood.

"He didn't die!" I shouted out. "He was murdered! I won't bury my father until someone comes up and admits this!"

Of course what I asked was ridiculous. I was a young girl in my twenties lacking experience and discretion. How could I think that any Communist would ever admit that my father was murdered. My mom started to cry.

Soon they came and took his body away. At the funeral parlor he was given a bath, his hair was cut, and he was placed where people could view him. Again I saw blood coming from his mouth, his nose, his eyes, and his ears.

Finally I said, "There will be no funeral. I will not let it begin until whoever gave him the medicine comes. Then I'll start the ceremony."

There was no place I could go to cry. There was no place to ask for justice, because we were not allowed to question the authorities.

The funeral director became quite excited because at three o'clock there was another funeral. I took a picture of my father and sent it to my grandfather in Brazil. I wanted the world to know about his death.

Finally the doctor who had given him the medicine did come and said the medicine was something like the name of sodium salicylate and it was for rheumatism and heart trouble. My father had neither, but they were testing the drug and he had been given too much and it killed him.

After the doctor had told me this, I cried and said, "All right, you can have the funeral now."

Everyone came to see my father, friends from miles away. They could see the blood seeping

My father's grave

from every opening of his body. *Oh, he was murdered*, I thought, over and over again. *If only I had known that morning this would be the last chance I would have to see him, I would have never left.* I was crying. I didn't like to think about how he died, all by himself. He didn't have anyone around him. And he was killed—by that medicine. We didn't have anywhere to go or anything to say. We could only take what happened and swallow it.

A month before the death of my father my second child, a daughter, was born. This made me feel worse. Oh, how I longed to get out of this place. I thought many nights, *I would rather die! This is no place for a human being to live.* Oh, how I pleaded to be a slave in a free country rather than to live like this. I said, "Lord, things are so hard. My father is gone, my mother has now had a heart attack and is so ill, and we don't have enough food. Please, God, make a way of escape!"

The only way we could buy food was with tickets. Nothing could be bought at the market without a ticket. Everything we ate was severely rationed. An egg became almost as valuable as a diamond. There was little meat to be had. Without ration tickets there was no food. If anyone dared to complain that there weren't enough tickets he only received less.

My husband was a large man and was therefore a big eater. I was really concerned about my mother or my baby starving. I just asked the Lord to help me eat less so that I could give more to my babies. I got so desperate; I didn't know what to do. I thought we would all die. I cried to the Lord, "Jesus, what are we going to do?"

He said to me, "Nora, would you believe me for one thing?"

I said, "Yes, Lord, for what?"

He said, "Trust me for only one day at a time. Nora, if you believe me, you must now send your daughter to your mother-in-law, who lives in Hong Kong."

My daughter was only twelve months old and would not be able to travel by herself. But the Lord put it in the heart of one of the women who was helping me to go with her, even though she had a son, a mother-in-law, and a husband on the mainland of China. She said she would go with my daughter to Hong Kong. How this amazed me! This truly was the hand of God! But when He opens the way, He also provides.

We applied for the visas, and in three short

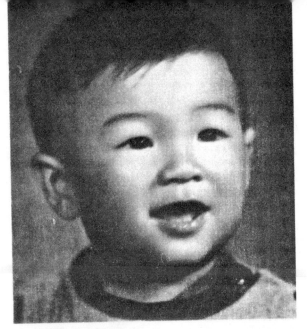

Paul - (My first-born)　　　　Ruth - (My daughter)

weeks the Communists allowed them to go to Hong Kong. I took them to Canton, a trip which took two days and three nights from Shanghai by train. How hard it was for me to send my daughter away! But she was really never very close to me for I was at the school much of the time and seldom at home. Although this woman had taken care of her more than I, during those two nights and three days on the train my daughter wanted me. They said this must have been instinct, knowing that she was going to leave her mother. That made it even harder for me to push her away from me, to see her leave by boat to Macao and on to Hong Kong.

I said good-bye to her and stood there crying after they left. They had only been gone briefly when they came back. The maid handed a small gold cross to me. Having been given it as a baby, the child was wearing her necklace. The sight of a cross would not help them to leave a Communist country.

I saw my daughter and my maid crying but I knew I had to obey God's orders. I felt this was the first test that God had prepared for my family to get out of China.

Several months later, men from the court where my husband worked came by and said they were going to send my husband into a labor center for physical labor training. It was their belief that all educated people should have labor experience. I knew that my husband had had tuberculosis when he was younger and that he had been very sick. One of his brothers was already dying of the disease. I knew if they put him under this kind of training he would soon die.

So I wrote to my mother-in-law and told her that I would rather have her son live with her than have him stay with me. I didn't want to see him die. At the time his father was dying of a liver problem, and that was a good excuse to apply for a permit. He would ask to visit his father for a month or so.

Of course there was no thought of his being released. But I was sure that as long as they realized his son and his wife remained behind that he would return, and that would be a guarantee that he would be back. Also, I was expecting my third child. They reasoned that every man would return home to be with his wife at the time of her delivery. I knew that I had to send him away to prolong his life rather than risk his death in a labor camp. So I told the Communists that I would be their assurance that he would return.

God's hand was with us again and the visa came through. By faith I said to my husband, "I don't know if I'll see you while I'm in my twenties, but we'll meet again someday."

I did ask him to do just one favor for me. "As soon as you get in Hong Kong, send me a telegram and say: 'Nora, would you please join me.'" He thought I'd gone crazy!

He said, "Do you think the Communists would let you go because I sent a telegram? You sent a daughter back, and now you send me back, and you want to get out? Don't be foolish! They'll never let you go!"

I said, "Well, don't you worry about the rest. Please! Just send the telegram!"

It was hard for me to send him away at the train station. I'll never forget that moment. It was on May 8, 1958 and our third baby was due in June. At the station as he left there were police and soldiers standing all around. I dared not cry. I could not express my feelings. I was holding my son Chuin Man in my arms. He was almost two years old but he couldn't talk or say good-bye. He didn't know how to speak. He could hardly walk because he was undernourished so I had to hold him. It was sad to see the train move out of the station, and the tears I had not allowed to come out were flowing inside of me.

I got home that night around seven o'clock, the train having left about two-thirty. There was a call from the school telling me to return. As I left I prayed, "Lord, I've asked my husband to send me a telegram." The telegram didn't come until seven days later. I was so discouraged. But the Lord had His purpose for allowing the delay in my receiving it. The Communists, I think, had realized that I was planning all these things to get out of Communist China, both the departures of my daughter and my husband. Now I wanted to go.

So they said, "Well, it will be nice for you to go through the labor experience which we require of all the educated people, and it will be especially nice since you are pregnant. It will make your birth easier. The work is hard."

Chapter Ten
OUT FROM RED CHINA

The next morning I was taken to the training center. The ride on the back of a truck was almost more than I could endure. I was eight months into my pregnancy and I was swollen with water. I weighed over 210 pounds, and it was hard for me even to walk normally. Packed into the truck with me were a load of students and teachers who were also going to feel the pangs of labor so they would not think intellectualism was the only way to success under the Communists. Ahead I saw a huge mountain of coal and the truck stopped. We were there.

I was given sacks and told to load them with coal and carry them from the coal mountain to the truck, and back again, back and forth. Of course, I didn't have any leather shoes. We make shoes of cloth—soles made of rags pasted on a board—so after a few days of this I was literally walking with barefeet. It was hard work walking up the hill and then down, unloading the coal on the truck, and going back and forth, back and forth. I had to walk over a rough, narrow wooden plank and often got splinters in my feet. Soon my feet were full of blisters and splinters.

But I was rather stubborn and, although it was hard, I didn't want to show my weakness in front of my enemies. I didn't want people to think I was a weak Christian. Because I didn't complain I was made to carry heavier and heavier loads weighing over a hundred pounds. Then it was time.

My nine months were up and the time for my baby to be delivered had come. A doctor checked me and couldn't understand why I hadn't already given birth under all this hard labor. Ah, but there was one thing he didn't know— God was with me!

My back pained me so much that at night, rather than to lie down, I would sit on the floor. I cried to God day and night asking for release from my suffering. I knew full well that when this child was born I would have at least fifty-six days of rest. Even the Communists allowed this break. I didn't know what to do. As I was sitting alone, suddenly I heard the voice of God speaking to me.

He said, "Nora, I'm with you. Your baby will never be born in Red Cina."

I thought, *God, that's ridiculous! I applied to the police for a visa and no one would even talk to me!* I knew the officials were waiting to see whether or not all this labor work would bring on the baby.

My whole back and shoulders were torn and bleeding, and my face was covered with boils, blisters, and sunburn. This was not the kind of suntan an American gets in his yard by a swimming pool. This was a very severe burn which would not heal because of daily exposure to the sun. My mouth was torn and bleeding and, of course, vitamin C was badly needed. I did not have enough food or water. Many times I would fall down, cry, and faint, but my Communist supervisors didn't say a thing. They just thought I was pretending. There was no rest, no smiles, just work. Carrying the bags of coal back and forth, back and forth.

It would have been hard enough for me in a normal state, but here I was pregnant and the baby was overdue. I couldn't get used to this, but every night I would hold on to the feet of Jesus like He was there. I would say, "Jesus, You are the only one that I cling to. And I know that you can do a miracle. Save me and bring me out from Red China."

As I was praying, I would literally feel the warmth of the feet of Jesus. I felt that He was there. I *knew* that He was there! And, oh, the comfort as I clung to Him. His strength would restore me. In the morning I could face another day. Day after day it was like this.

It was June now, and almost every day I would go to the police station and ask if my visa to get out of China had come through. Then July came, and August. Nine, ten, eleven months, and the baby was still there, moving up and down. I couldn't understand what was going on.

Then the Lord spoke to me again. He said, "Nora, the baby is alive and well in your womb. And I am with you. You need not be afraid. Nora, your child is assigned to me, the Lord. And as long as this child is in your womb, it is a sign that I am with you. Rest assured, this child will be born, but on free soil."

It was during my twelfth month of pregnancy on one of the mornings that I was sitting in the office. A voice spoke to me. Immediately I knew it was the Lord because it was so strong and clear. "Nora, the way is now open. I've prepared the path. You will be getting out of China."

Quickly I picked up the phone and called my mother. But she wasn't able to come to the phone. She was dying of heart trouble and I told the one who answered the phone, "You have to get my mother to the phone. This is urgent!"

I said, "Mom, I'm leaving tomorrow." She asked how I knew. I said, "The Lord has told me. Mom, tomorrow I'm leaving. God will also provide a way for you."

I picked up the phone to call the police station. You people in America can call the sheriff any time and they come right to your door, but in a Communist country, especially when you apply for a visa, you are not to call the police. So when I called, the Lord gave me courage. I recognized the voice of the man who answered. I had met him twice and I called him by name.

He said, "If you want to know anything about your visa, come in this afternoon about four."

The Lord said to me, "No, go there at two. It's urgent."

I checked with the airlines; they are not like airlines in the United States—United, TWA, Eastern, and American—in Red China there was one airline, the Communist. First I was asked if I had a visa. Then I was told there were only two flights from Shanghai to Canton, Wednesday and Friday. This was Tuesday, so I thought if I don't catch the Wednesday flight, I'll have to wait until Friday. I said that I wanted to book a flight for tomorrow, Wednesday. I believed that God's directions were to be followed by immediate action.

So I went to the police station at two, not four o'clock. The head of the police came to see me. He was a man in a very high position, and he had a very mean face. He said to me, "You sent forty telegrams, to Mao Tse-tung and to Chou En Lai. You've complained that we Communists spread propaganda that we'll allow freedom to anyone, and then we didn't allow you to get out. It's especially bad that you're using that old gimmick of giving birth to a baby and that you have fifty-six days of vacation and want to use them to get out of China to visit your relatives. We haven't allowed you to do so, of course. So now Peking is checking up on Shanghai to find out why we don't allow you to leave. We were blamed. You have made too big a noise in Peking to Chou En Lai! [He was, at the time, the one responsible for letting people out.] You have put us in a bad spot. We usually require our people to come back when we allow them to visit relatives, but you are an exception. We want you to get out—not only get out—but stay out!"

He threw the passport at me; I took it and left. Rushing home, I packed my few belongings. It was hard to leave because now I had to say good-bye to my elderly mother who was dying, and leave her alone with my twelve-year-old brother.

I can remember that I looked longingly at my mother as she lay there in the bed. I was thinking, *Perhaps this is the last time that my eyes will see her on this earth.* Yet for some strange reason, I knew that God in His mercy would somehow deliver her. I cried and cried. But soon the time of my departure came. I recall my last words to her: "Mother, somehow I know Jesus will allow us to meet again."

I had no chance to take anything along. Every part of our bodies was searched. In fact, they even told me to leave my wedding ring behind. As I prepared to leave the land and walk across the desert area called No Man's Land, it became almost more than I could bear. I was so huge and heavy, and my son wasn't able to walk very well. We didn't have good shoes either. But, how wonderful it was as we began our walk across that barren land to realize that on the other side was freedom. I was filled with praise to God for the very thought: *freedom was now in our grasp.*

My mind went back to those days when I'd gone through a situation almost like this during my childhood—walking to freedom from the Japanese. Now here I was, once again fleeing from my own people.

The land was hard and parched with broken glass and branches and brush. Soon our legs were torn and bleeding. We had no food or water to sustain us as we walked, alone in the heat. The desolation of those hours! I can't even remember how far it was, or how long the walk took. But it was so hot, and the ground was so rough, that we both fell many times. This was the hardest journey that I had ever been on in my life.

Soon after we started walking, I began to bleed. I fell to my knees and cried to the Lord, "Now, Lord, this is the end of the line. If the baby is born here in the desert, I will die and so will he. Please—Spirit of God, help us!" Now, as I remember, I doubt if the journey was more than a mile's distance, but it seemed endless. I would fall and resolve not to get up again. But then my little son would beg me, tug on my clothes, and I would get up. Then Chuin Man would become so tired he would beg me to carry him, but I

Chuin Man 3 months old

Ready to leave China

101

couldn't. I needed someone to hold me. I was cut and swollen and my son's legs and feet were bleeding. We had been traveling for hours.

I begged the Lord to prevail and bring this son to the land of freedom. It was worth all the suffering to hold his little hand and encourage him to walk. "Just one more step at a time, please God, let this little boy walk," I prayed. I thank the Lord how He encouraged me; when I fell, He would use that little boy, that little hand, to pull on my dress. Chuin Man thought that he had such strength that he could pull my body up. Little did he know that it was by the tug of that little hand that God lifted me up to new strength. He gave me healing strength to go on.

Finally we could see the border ahead and the people there waiting to see if their friends or a loved one had gotten out. Strangers offered us bread and food to eat. When we finally arrived in Macao we both cried for hours without stopping. Neither ice cream nor toys could stop the little boy's crying. People offered us anything they could get hold of to feed these two hungry refugees. How thankful we were!

But nothing stopped Chiun Man from crying. He was literally screaming, like a man having a nervous breakdown, from the pressure he had just been through. I picked up a handful of dirt and let it run through my fingers. I thought, *Lord, this is the land where I can have the freedom to worship You.* I breathed the free air into my lungs and was thankful to the Lord. He had provided a place for us to breathe in this freedom. I could once again worship Him without fear of death. Through my tears I rejoiced that God had truly proved that *He was my strength and my refuge.*

Chapter Eleven
CHILD OF PROMISE

Macao was by no means the end of my journey. I knew that the place for me to go was Hong Kong, forty miles away. I was anxious to cross the bay from Macao to Hong Kong as the labor pains of childbirth had begun.

My husband wasn't to meet me in Macao because he didn't have any identification from the Hong Kong government at that time. Without proper identification he couldn't cross by boat from Hong Kong. Fortunately my husband's brother and wife were able to meet Chuin Man and me in Macao.

I will always remember Macao because it was full of gambling casinos. Many people went there every weekend and lost their money. They would even gamble on the boat crossing the bay. Most of the dealers were girls. There was free food and free drink when you gambled. To see all that food and drink available was new to me, because I had just gotten out of China. The worst problem was that I didn't speak the same dialect as the people from Hong Kong so I couldn't communicate with them. I spoke Mandarin and Shanghai dialect and they spoke Cantonese.

I waited for more than seven days in Macao before I was finally smuggled into Hong Kong. Most of the people escaping from Red China had to be smuggled into Hong Kong. But as long as you got identification papers, nobody would bother you.

One way of escaping was to be smuggled out in a small sailing boat. The refugee would have to curl up in the hold like a snake. For this discomfort one would pay two hundred Hong Kong dollars. The risk was great and many were drowned or suffocated on the journey. If he were caught he would be sent back from Hong Kong to the terror of Communist punishment.

Oh, how worried I was! My baby was overdue and I was really upset. I said, "Lord, if all the time You wanted me to come here and have my baby born in Macao—I'd rather go back to Red China. My mother's there. I don't have anybody here. Oh, don't let me have my baby here alone. You told me you didn't want me to have the baby in Red China, and I believe you don't want it born here!"

I was so large. I couldn't communicate with anyone. The weather was so hot; it was August. I could hardly breathe because of the oppressive heat and my enormous size. Everything seemed hopeless and I was tired and sick. The day finally came when I was told it was my turn to leave for Hong Kong. The delay was longer, so my father-in-law had to pay more and more money to get my son and myself out of Macao. They altered my papers so that I could use them to get into Hong Kong.

Finally we got on the boat. I don't want to reveal the details of how I was smuggled out, because I don't want to jeopardize anyone else's chances of escape from Red China into Hong Kong.

At this last stage of the escape there were no relatives with us; we were brought to the boat by a stranger. I was on the boat for three or four hours. Many things were troubling me. I was having trouble with the language. This was my first experience with the Cantonese dialect, which was just like a foreign language to me.

What would I do? When my boat landed and I got off, how would I manage? I would have to have somebody stamp my papers to allow me to enter Hong Kong legally.

When I got there, the police stopped me. I don't know exactly what took place, but I think the legal matters had been arranged. I got off the boat and was allowed into Hong Kong.

Once more, I realized God had made a way for me. I was greeted there by two or three cars and a gathering of people: my husband, my husband's family, my father-in-law, and other members of the family.

I must have looked almost like a beggar after that difficult trip. Suddenly I became aware of all the luxury around me—there were cars and well-dressed people everywhere.

We got into the car and left in a hurry. I found out later that even after I was in the car I could be caught and taken away. No one wanted to take any further chances of my being sent out of Hong Kong. The car didn't stop until we arrived at my in-laws' home. It was a three-story, old-fashioned Chinese house with two stone lions guarding the entrance to the front door—a beautiful home. The bottom flats were rented to others. I would live on the second floor and my in-laws lived on the third. When I went inside it was cool and comfortable. There are no words to express how grateful I was to God for supplying me with this air-conditioned environment.

In the Chinese tradition, when you are married into your husband's family you must go into the family and serve them tea at the wedding. We weren't married in Hong Kong but in China, so we hadn't done this. The moment we got into the home they put two chairs in front of us. My father-in-law and my mother-in-law sat down, and my husband and I had to pour tea for them even though we long ago had been married. Then they gave me four bars of gold, worth $1,200 in Hong Kong dollars, to receive me into the Lam family.

The maid who had taken my daughter out of China was the only one close to me. She was also the one person I could talk to in my own dialect. She told me my daughter, who was twelve months old when they arrived, had become a popular child. My maid told me wonderful stories about how well they had cared for her and treated her.

I was especially eager to learn the story of how she and my daughter had arrived in Macao and been smuggled out. Their problem was not getting the baby in, but finding someone to accompany her. The Hong Kong government had a rule at the time that a baby who could be carried was not required to have a Hong Kong residence certificate to enter. Since my daughter had been taken care of by this one woman all her life, she was happy as long as they were together.

When the two arrived at Macao my two sisters-in-law took charge of the situation. They decided to cross the harbor right away and took the small child from her nanny. Their plans were to smuggle the child on a small boat; they had only paid $200 for her smuggling fee.

The baby started to cry from fright. She didn't want these people. She scratched their faces and pulled their hair. The only one my daughter wanted was her nanny, who was called Grace in American and Ah Hsing in Chinese. Suddenly Grace was left standing alone and the baby disappeared with these two strange women into the crowds of people. Crying all the way, she was brought to my husband's family.

Unfortunately Grace wasn't the only one who was escaping. Thousands of people were waiting to get to Hong Kong. She spent two nights in Macao before being smuggled out in a *sampan* with thirteen other people. She could hardly breathe, they were packed in so tightly. Sometimes the trip was so long that the people would die. They couldn't get on the deck in time for air because they didn't want the police to see them. Police on sea patrol searched the boats to see if they were carrying smugglers. Some people treated the refugees like pigs. Conditions were terrible: no talking, no food, no bathroom. When they got out of the boat they had to walk and walk and even sometimes run until a truck could pick them up. Then they were squeezed inside—so nobody could see them. She said that if she had known she would be given this kind of treatment she would have never wanted to come.

Grace was anxious to tell me all the details about the trip. She and I were about the same age and understood each other. Besides, since leaving Communist China, Grace had been unable to speak to anyone. The language spoken in the street was strange to her. Because she had grown up as a farmer, she had not been taught to read or write.

In her effort to get to Hong Kong to rejoin the baby she ran into trouble. First of all, she was very conspicuous on the street. People from the mainland didn't wear make-up or have their hair done and their clothes were not good. People could tell in a minute that Grace was from Red China. The smuggler leader had to tell her to change clothes. In case she was stopped it might help her to look like the others.

Finally Grace arrived at Kowloon, opposite Hong Kong, and was instructed to run. She got on a very small bus. The other people inside were packed close together, but nobody spoke. The bus driver drove them as fast as he could to another place and told them to get out. Grace changed clothes there and crossed the border to the city of Hong Kong. She was smuggled in and arrived near midnight.

She said that from the minute she walked into my mother-in-law's house she could not communicate with these people. Her first concern was to ask where the baby was. She finally understood that the baby was on the third floor. The minute her voice carried from the ground floor to the third floor, the baby woke up. Chiun Way started to cry because she wanted the maid to hold her and from then on would hardly let anybody else touch her.

My mother-in-law told Grace to take a bath. She did as she was told but didn't enjoy it. The room for this use was at the top of the house, in the unheated servants' quarters. The weather was very cold, since the time of year was almost December, right before the Chinese New Year.

Her ordeal was over—the difficult experience of being smuggled in. But Hong Kong was strange to her and she found it hard to get used to. Hong Kong was a large city of over four million people and was growing daily. All the peoples of the world seemed to have businesses in Hong Kong, the crossroads of the Far East.

Everything was especially hard on me because my baby was expected at any minute. Here again I was completely dependent on others—I couldn't speak the language and we had no money and therefore we had to accept all that they gave us. When I'd escaped from Red China, I was sure that a whole new way of life would be mine, but this wasn't quite what I had expected. Since both my husband and I were graduated from law school, I thought it would be much easier than it was to get started again. However, there were too many refugees all trying to make a new start. There wasn't much need for lawyers. Furthermore, our diplomas were not recognized in Hong Kong. We didn't have money to buy furniture and so we had to sleep on whatever we could find. But even so, it was freedom!

One of the major problems that I was facing was my baby's birth. I didn't know a doctor and it was rather difficult for me to share with anybody that I'd carried this child for twelve months. My mother-in-law finally took me to see a doctor. Soon the labor pains started and I was sent to the hospital only to discover that it was a false alarm. My brief stay in the hospital had been very costly and my mother-in-law was upset at the expense. The doctor told me to go home again. I thought, *Why am I going through this testing again? God, is something wrong? Have I failed You somehow?* Then eventually two weeks later the pain became bad, but I didn't want to tell anyone. I wanted to make sure that this time the baby would be born. Finally I knew I had to go to the hospital. For thirty-six hours I was in hard labor. This birth was the hardest I had. I thought, *If only my mother could be near me.*

My husband was there, but since I had arrived from China he'd been acting very strange and had been cruel and mean to me. I couldn't quite understand this, and I was puzzled and confused. I realize as I write this book that my life seems so pathetic and so full of burdens. But it was wonderful, even through all this, to see how the Lord was preparing me for a day yet ahead!

Oh, how glad I was when they brought my new little, fat son to me! Then my in-laws were happy because the new baby was a son! We named him Chuin Mo. Immediately there were phone calls to make informing all the relatives and friends. To a Chinese family a son is very important.

Twenty-four hours after I'd given birth to my new son, a rash developed all over me. I suppose it was from being overtired and rundown. I was in the hospital a week and then I went home with the baby to live with my in-laws. It was rather difficult because we had three babies to support. So I decided I'd have to go out and get a job. I rationalized that it was my fate in life, and I didn't care. I hated to live like a rich lady having people wait on me. I just couldn't stand to live under another person's roof and do nothing. I started to pray and look to God to learn what I should do next.

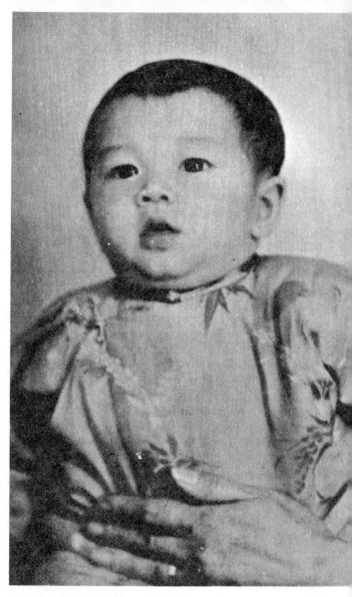

Joseph - (My child of promise)

Chapter Twelve
MOTHER

My mother was more fortunate than most Chinese because she had been well-educated. After studying six years in Chinese secondary schools, she finished her education in an American mission school. Because she wanted to attend this school and would be looked on with more favor by the teacher, she became a "rice Christian." At that time she did not know the Lord but it was easy to say that she would accept Jesus.

A small woman of not even five feet in height, my mother was a lady who had never known what it was to work. Her favorite pastime was playing mahjong, the most popular game in China. Many days she would play for sixteen hours.

It worried me when she lost lots of money. At this time she didn't have that much money to waste. I really believe that this kind of mahjong gambling has a spirit in it. You can't quit. It reminds one of many who say they can quit smoking or drinking, but they don't. There's a spirit that prevents them from stopping. Even though she knew she was wasting time and that it was bad for her, she still wanted to play, win or lose. As a little girl I worried about my mother—that my father would come back and scold her for gambling. I was told that if the pillow she slept on was stood up straight she would win. Every time she went out to play mahjong I would arrange her pillow believing that it would protect her. I tried to pray and ask God to help her. I would do anything to keep her from losing money. And now there she was—alone and suffering behind the Bamboo Curtain.

One night as I was praying, I saw the Lord and He promised me that my mother would get out of Red China. I wanted to believe this but knew how impossible, humanly speaking, it was. My mother had suffered a blockage in her heart, and for thirteen months hadn't even been able to take a bath alone. "Lord, how can she ever get out?" I prayed.

I was working now at an evangelistic center in Hong Kong called the New Life Temple. One of my responsibilities was to pass out tracts and booklets provided by Oral Roberts and others. To do this we drove out of the city in trucks, heading for Aberdeen where we would witness to the *sampan* dwellers. Because there is not enough ground for all the people to live on, the *sampan* people live night and day on the water. They never land; their home is the boat. Thousands of human beings live this way, with often an entire family on one boat: grandmother, daughter-in-law, grandson. Sometimes up to ten or more people live on this small, crowded sailing boat with strange-looking sails.

How well I remember January fourth, 1960. Almost the entire youth group of the church went down to the waterfront to pass out literature. We were all so happy. We had almost finished passing out all of our tracts and everybody was about ready to go home when I stood on the wharf to hand out the remainder of the tracts among the *sampans*. It was strange, but in China most people thought that coming to know Jesus meant being supplied with various material needs. Most of the people needed either money or food. The people in the *sampans* thought we were going to give them something to eat. Everybody was just pushing, trying to get a handout. They didn't know that the gospel book was words.

I was hit by somebody in the chest, and I fell twenty-feet below into the sea. At noon the sea is lower because the tide is out, so there were many stones exposed. Half of my body fell into water and half hit the rocks, and I was knocked unconscious. I was taken by ambulance to the emergency room of the Queen Mary hospital. I didn't know what had happened to me. I couldn't remember. When I regained my consciousness there was a cast on my left foot and a big knot on my head, and I seemed to be bleeding

117

all over. People started to laugh at me: "How come," somebody said, "your God didn't hold you up in the middle of your accident? You were working for 'the Living God,' how come this happened to you?"

They must have thought that Christians could never be attacked by the devil. I couldn't give them a good answer, but I remembered one thing. God's Word says that "God causes all things to work together for good to those who love God." I did serve the Lord and I loved Him. I worked many hours at the church. I thought, *There's no reason for the Lord to give us death as punishment, but I'm sure that this is working out for His good.* So I just lay there praising Jesus, waiting for good to come from my fall. In all my days I would never have dreamed that this accident would bring about my own mother's release from the Communists behind the Bamboo Curtain.

Three days later my true consciousness came back. At ten o'clock in the morning the wind started to blow the curtains gently and I heard the voice of God clearly say to me, "Nora, now is the time for your mother to come out of Red China. She will be with you soon."

Well, I knew that my mother was dying of heart trouble and that she couldn't travel that far—not like I had traveled. She couldn't even get out of the house. How could she travel? Because I hadn't heard from her that often, I didn't know whether or not she was suffering at the hands of the communists or what was going on. But she was. Every night interrogators came, asking if her daughter was coming back. "How come you haven't heard from your daughter?"

That she didn't die under this mental torment was a miracle in itself. Despite apparent impossibilities, I hung on to what Jesus promised me—that one day my mother would be out of Red China. So when the Holy Spirit spoke to me and said, *Now is the time when your mother will get out*, I immediately took action.

To listen to the voice and not to act would serve no purpose. An idea came into my mind. I remembered that the woman who had brought my daughter out of Red China was very strong. In fact, she used to carry over a hundred pounds of dirt on her shoulders and still walk fast. I asked her if she could carry me. I was so big she couldn't put me on her back, but she did pick me up in her arms and carry me downstairs.

It also occurred to me that I could try to get my mother released to help her daughter. If I could get evidence that I was injured, perhaps I could claim to the authorities I was crippled. Calling a taxi, I went immediately to the Queen Mary Hospital and the emergency room. It wasn't hard to get an X-ray report and a written report of my medical diagnosis and treatment. From the newspapers I cut out accounts of my accident.

Hopefully I sent off all this information to Red China authorities asking for my mother's release. Weeks went by and I had no word from my mother. *What's wrong*, I wondered, because I was certain she wanted desperately to leave Red China.

About six weeks later, in the middle of February, the cast was taken off and more X-rays taken. The doctor came out from the X-ray room and said, "I am very sorry that we were in such a hurry. The cast I put on your leg positioned the bone wrong. Your bone must be rebroken."

I cried out inwardly to the Lord, "Jesus! Why, Jesus, why?" I didn't know what was wrong. I went home and wept for a long time. I just couldn't understand what was happening. The plaster had been on for six weeks and it didn't do any good. Now they had to rebreak it? Rebreak my leg and set it again? I would be in a cast again. The Lord very quietly said to me, "Nora, have I ever left you alone? Have I ever failed you? How come you always lash out at me, Nora? Haven't I promised you that all things will work out for the good?" I answered quickly, "Jesus, what's this good for? I can't see any point in this. I only see misery and pain, and people laughing at me. Not only that I'm suffering so much, but if I have another cast put on, they'll laugh and tease me more because I have a weak God. What can you accomplish by this? I just don't understand!"

To make matters worse, my relatives came and laughed at me. They all pointed their finger at me—kind of accusing, you know. I started to really get down to business with God. And I said, "God, show me what you want me to do." The Lord replied, "Go back, have another operation and send another set of reports to your mother." I didn't know it at the time, but she hadn't used the first set of documents to get out. She thought I was making up a story, and didn't think it would work. When this happened the second time, she started to realize my claim was true.

The second operation took place in March. I'll always remember all the certified documents that went back to China. Sometime in May the cast was taken off and I got up on my own feet again. It was just like walking on thousands of needles and I couldn't put on shoes. That again made me so discouraged.

The pastor came by one day and brought me a crutch. I didn't have enough money to buy one at that time. He said to me, "You'd better come back to church tomorrow to work." I said, "Pastor, for heaven's sake, how can I come to work? I don't have any transportation. We don't have a car. I have to take the street car which is always crowded, often with only standing room." He said, "I'll try to pick you up so that you can come back to church." That was very important, because when the workers get discouraged and cut off their fellowship with other Christians they get more discouraged. That's the reason it is so hard to be a Christian in a communist country— because the Christians are so cut off from fellowship with other Christians.

I told him that I had a mother who was trapped behind the Bamboo Curtain. I asked the church to pray for my mother in every prayer meeting. Every day I prayed for my mother's release from Red China.

That was in May, and then June came, July, and August. Oh, how long those months seemed! I kept remembering those words that the Spirit of God had spoken to me, "Now is the time for your mother to come out."

"Then why—why, God? Why have these months passed so slow? You told me so long ago that my mother would be freed."

One day I was working in the church and

praying as always. We were in the midst of a revival, and I'd come home about ten o'clock. I was so tired I threw my body on the couch and fell asleep. Then an angel of God appeared to me and said, "Nora, Nora, wake up!" I woke up and noticed it was three o'clock in the morning. The reason I looked at the clock was because people often laughed at me when I told them of these spiritual experiences. They wanted me to tell them when and where they happened. They would mock, "There's Nora, who says she believes in supernatural happenings." The angel of God said to me, "Nora, it's tomorrow. Tomorrow, your mother will be here. Rest assured —she will arrive."

I was so excited that I woke up my husband, my children, the maid, the neighbors, and called my girl friends to share with them what the voice of God had told me through His messenger—that my mother was coming tomorrow from Red China. All these months I hadn't heard a word from my mother. She had never sent me a card or a letter. I didn't even know if she had applied to get out or not. I knew nothing! But I knew the voice was directly from God because I saw the angel in person. So the next day when I woke up, I ran into town immediately and I borrowed a hundred dollars Hong Kong money to buy a set of furniture. I bought a desk, a bed, and a chest of drawers. I also rented a room in an apartment for eighty dollars Hong Kong money a month. I went into action, believing Hebrews 11:1, which says: "Now faith is the assurance of things hoped for, the conviction of things not seen." If you have to see everything, touch everything, the blessing is not as great as when you act in pure faith. So, in faith I rented the apartment and bought the furniture.

I was expecting to see my mother that very day. I went to church to work. They were still having the crusade and I couldn't come home until 10:30 P.M. The preacher was still preaching when it reached 10:30. When I got home I thought something was wrong with the children. I didn't know that there was a telegram lying on the table. It said, "I'm on my way to you, Nora. Signed Mother." The telegram was sent from Macao. That was only forty miles away. "She is in Macao! She is already out!" I cried, "Oh yes, I told you that at three o'clock in the morning God told me she was coming, only nobody believed me." My family had considered me to be sick—a mental case, in fact, when I had made my announcement at 3 A.M. That I could be so sure of what God told me would come to pass was unbelievable to them. I was someone odd: the one who spoke in a strange tongue during my time in prayer, who had an accident—probably fell down the stairs so hard that she damaged her brain!

Just then something strange happened in the kitchen; I heard something crash to the floor. I ran in to see what was wrong. There stood the maid, Yee Ah Hsing, who had brought my daughter out of China. She had taken a little Buddha with her, and had it hidden in the kitchen. Now she had broken it into many pieces. "Mrs. Lam," she cried to me, "I don't want to believe in that kind of god anymore. Mrs. Lam, I want

123

to believe in your God as my God. I will accept your Jesus as my Jesus." So we prayed and she repented.

She was the first convert of my ministry, a ministry which started after that right in my home. The moment I laid my hands on her and told her about Jesus, the Holy Spirit fell upon her. She received Jesus and broke out speaking in a heavenly language.

Finally Mother arrived. She told me later she didn't know how she could travel. But when her time came for her visa, she said the power came down from somewhere and she had strength to start on the trip. She said that the moment she got out of the car, it stopped raining, but when she got in the car it would start to rain again. "When I needed strength I had it, I just couldn't believe it. God must have had something to do with my escape."

But though she had been delivered by God and was in Hong Kong, that old urge to play mahjong, that temptation, came back upon her again. That root, that seed began to grow.

It was Christmas Day and she had decided to go to church with me. I didn't realize that she had a mahjong party all set up for that afternoon. She didn't come home from church with us for lunch, but crossed the harbor to Kowloon to play mahjong. She got home very late that night and the next day she was desperately sick. I called the doctor for her immediately; she almost didn't survive. The Lord was teaching her a lesson because she didn't follow the way the Lord wanted her to go.

It was very hard for her to change. I really

hated the gambling, but she couldn't understand how I felt because she liked mahjong. Later on, when she got well, she gambled again. I tell you, it was the big thing in her life. We are Christians and we think we are living a good life, but if we are not really living to win people to Christ or doing anything for the Lord, it's not enough.

One day a big lesson came into my mother's life. It was in 1964 and she had a stroke. We had to take her to the Queen Mary Hospital, unconscious, and there she lay for many days and nights. She would regain consciousness only to pass out again. She was in and out of consciousness and we were all sure she was going to die. The doctor told us once that she was three hours away from death. He told us to prepare for the funeral. I got alone in a room and cried out to the Lord. "Lord, if this is the last chance for her to live again, I want her to live to experience You alone and not material things. She has had everything before, but she didn't know You as a person. Oh Lord, forgive her and heal her."

While I was praying, the doctor was treating my mother for heart trouble and high blood pressure. "When a person has these two diseases together," the doctor said, "it is difficult to prescribe medicine. If I use one injection it will affect her brain and she'll be a mental case. If I give her pills for her heart, she'll die."

That was the moment I called upon the church, and many of my dear brothers and sisters started to pray. After the fourth day of praying and fasting her consciousness started to come back. In a few weeks she was released from the hospital. In only one year she could walk normally, just as if she hadn't had a stroke or been lame. She understood at last that this long illness was a lesson from God. If God had been so good, she realized, He must really love her greatly. But she still couldn't obey God in the way He wanted her to.

I immigrated to the United States in 1967 and telegraphed her to come also when I got settled there. I had been speaking and traveling, and I needed her to be with my children. She made arrangements and joined me in America after awhile.

Although my mother's health had come back after her almost fatal sickness, she also suffered from arthritis for over thirty years. Every night she woke up to rub her neck and put ointment on it. This brought her only temporary relief; for arthritis there is no cure.

Each time she went to see a heart specialist for heart trouble, the cost would be close to a hundred dollars. The doctor would say, "I'm sorry. We can't help her." At that time she only weighed eighty pounds. She couldn't even swallow. I said, "Lord, if I ever needed a mother I need one right now because I don't have anyone else in this strange land." I said, "Please, save her life and let her experience your Spirit and healing."

One day Mom came back from the doctor and I told her, "Mom, there is now no other hope in the world for you unless you yield yourself to Jesus and let Him heal you. If you read the Bible so often and it hasn't become a reality to you, it's no use."

She got down to business with the Lord. She knelt down and prayed, asking God to help her. One day she came home from church and claimed

126

to be healed. She had gone so many times for prayer, but she never before knew she was healed. Tonight she said, "Nora, I was healed." I said, "How do you know?" She said, "I just know. I feel it all over my body." From that day on she started to gain weight. She now weighs a hundred and five pounds and no longer has arthritis or heart trouble. She had a doctor check her later, and the doctor said her heart had no problems anymore.

For thirty years she's had high blood pressure with her upper being over 200 and the lower 100. Now at the age of seventy-two her blood pressure is 130/80, just like that of a young girl. The Lord restored her—not only to let her know that He was real and enable her to become closer to Him—but for her own well-being. She's as healthy as she can be now. She goes to church many times a week, witnesses for the Lord and loves the Lord with all her heart. How thankful I am for a precious "China doll" mother.

Chapter Thirteen
WISDOM FROM GOD

I worked at an evangelistic center in Hong Kong for over two years. Many things had happened to me, as I related before: I had fallen into the sea, and my mother had been released from Red China. Now I had the added responsibility of feeding and clothing my mother. We didn't have much money but, enough.

After a while, God seemed to speak to me about finding a different job. I had a degree from Red China, but nobody would hire me. The British government did not recognize my degree or any other degrees from Red China. The Lord had different plans; He opened a new way.

Soon I found myself as a school teacher, teaching a class of fifth graders. That was a miracle in itself because people from Red China hardly ever get a teaching certificate from the British government. The permits I had should have been useless but God planned otherwise. I taught in the school for one year and what a blessing it was.

In 1960 I saw in the paper an ad for a social worker for the city of Hong Kong. I'd always loved contacts with people. This job seemed like such a tremendous opening for me to be a witness to so many. There were drawbacks. My English was bad, and it would be very hard for me to take any test for the position. In my heart I knew it would be impossible for me to qualify. I thought of all the reports that I would have to fill out—yet my burden for this work was great. I thought that I could be of help to many of the thousands of refugees coming out of Red China every day and pouring like a flood into the city of Hong Kong. What should I do?

Then I thought, *If the Lord is willing to help me, He can do everything. I'll just trust Him.* So I applied for the job. I wondered if this step was brave, or just foolhardy.

When I got to the office and filled out my application it was put with others made by more eligible graduates from the Hong Kong University seeking the same job. I knew that they would have priority in getting the best jobs.

At that time I found out the pay was going to be $560 Hong Kong money a month and I had only been getting $150 Hong Kong money at the church and my teaching salary was $350

Hong Kong money. So the $560 Hong Kong money seemed like a fortune. I was anxious to get into the work where I could exercise the experience and the power of God. I believed the Lord could give me wisdom. After all, didn't He delay the birth of my son for three months? I knew that many people thought I was crazy to trust God for something that seemed so impossible. They told me that I would just make a fool of myself and God.

It's a wonderful blessing and joy when we really put our faith in the Lord and give Him everything. For some strange reason I knew that the Lord would see me through at this time. I didn't have a single doubt. I didn't know then that there would be two tests for the job—written and oral. When I found that out my faith was really tested. I thought, *Well, it's just impossible for me to do this written test. My English is terrible—it doesn't allow me to coordinate my thoughts compared to the University students that are here. And the oral test!—How can I ever communicate?* Then I thought, *If I don't walk into the sea it will never part.* So I said, "Lord, I'm going to take the test and You must help me."

Now I really applied myself. I studied night and day, pouring over books from the Post Office with facts about Hong Kong. Soon I knew important details like the size, population, and a great deal about its people. The Lord even revealed to me the most important questions that would be asked on the test.

One of the first questions on the exam would be to tell the reason why I wanted to join the Social Welfare Department. The second was a case study of a *Sampan* family. I could hardly believe it that these two questions were exactly the same as the Lord had earlier revealed to me that I should prepare for. I know many of you reading this book will think this ridiculous but it really happened.

A tutor by the name of Mr. Tong helped me to learn other information for the Welfare Department such as where and how to apply, what books to read, and other things. For three days I talked to no one but God, and I studied hard. Then the day came for me to take the written test.

I had a friend living in Hong Kong who had graduated from St. John's University in Shanghai and was at that time working for the telephone company. She was also going to take the test. Her English was far better than mine, and she knew more about Hong Kong because she had lived there for many years. I had only been there for three years.

While I was in the waiting room before the test was to be given, I saw Hong Kong University students who were also applicants. They all looked elegant, and talked almost perfect English. It would only be natural that they would want to hire students from their own University. I didn't have anywhere to turn but to God.

I said, "Lord, you sent me here and they are going to ask me what university I graduated from." I was so scared, I didn't even dare to share my fright with anyone.

Sure enough, soon they asked me how long I had been in Hong Kong and where I had been schooled. These questions were routinely asked before the test was given. My English was poor, and I didn't know if they understood me or not. Afterward I sat in the corner alone and didn't talk to anyone.

Then they called us to take the test. It would last three hours and there could be no talking. We would not be allowed to ask any questions.

"Now Lord," I said, "I'm going to pray. I understand that in the old days when the prophets wrote the Bible, that the Spirit wrote through them. Now, if You want me to enter this social welfare department, Jesus, You are the One who will have to help me write the answers. I'm going to sit still and pray. Please give me the words I should write down."

People started to write, I prayed: "Lord, help me to remember all that I have studied, and to write the answers down. Thank You, Jesus."

Then a miracle took place! I started writing down the answers. In fifty minutes I had answered all the questions and I was finished. I didn't see any reason to sit there anymore, so I just got up, handed in my test and left.

I said, "Lord, I've done my job and You have done Yours. Together we have done the impossible." I found out later from my girl friend, that no one but me had left before the three hours were up. I thought, *Oh my goodness, maybe everything is wrong. If these other people stayed for three hours and I finished in fifty minutes, I don't have a chance.*

The Lord said to me, "Now, Nora, I told you what to do and you did it. It was all you could do."

A few weeks later, I was called for another interview.

I went to the head of the department and met the Principal of the Child Welfare section, Miss Jenny Cheung. During the interview I shared with her the feelings in my heart. I had written down lots of words on the test that I didn't even remember now. It was Jesus who helped me to remember all those things that I studied so that I was able to pass. She was a Roman Catholic, I found out.

She said, "Nora, I knew that, for some reason I wanted to interview you." She hadn't even met me before the interview and here God was talking with her heart. She told me that I should get one more minister to give me a reference and that I would probably get the job. I did this and then prepared to take the health exam.

Several days later I received a telephone call telling me that I had been given the job. I was now a welfare worker. I got to visit the children of hundreds of families that were poor and needed help desperately.

It was a wonderful experience to share Jesus with so many of them. I soon found out that feeding and helping people physically is not the only answer. It is only a minor help to human beings, to feed their stomachs. The main need of every man is Jesus.

In 1961 there were floods of people trying to get over the border into Hong Kong. They were escaping over the mountains, through the rivers, and in any possible way—just to reach freedom. Many died during their escape attempt. It was such a tragedy. Refugees roamed around the city like dogs, thirsty and hungry with nowhere to go.

Then the day came that barriers were put up and refugees were no longer allowed to come into Hong Kong.

None of the government servants were allowed to aid, support, or comfort these refugees who were waiting at the border. Even if a member of your own family was among those newly arrived we had to turn our backs on them. There were so many hundreds of thousands of them trying to get across the border that everything became confusion. Most of the police and most of the government workers were sent to the border to try and keep order. The British government had tried to take care of each refugee as much as possible. Refugee centers had been set up, but soon it became impossible to handle the number of people that were coming across the border. There wasn't enough water, food, or proper sanitation. There were not enough jobs. To let them continue to pour in like this would only mean sickness and death for those trying to reach freedom. The barriers reminded me how fortunate I was to have been freed. I couldn't stand it—the misery of so many people.

With all this conflict going on in my soul of not being able to help those who desperately needed help through the channels in which I worked, I decided I had better quit my job. It was breaking my heart.

"What do You have in store for me now Lord?" I wondered.

Chapter Fourteen
FULLNESS OF THE SPIRIT

There were a lot of different denominations and churches in Hong Kong and some people would tell me to go to this church, and then some other church. I finally said, "Hold on. I got out of China by the power of God and I want to find a church that doesn't just make a show out of shaking hands and having a beautiful building. These things can no longer satisfy me."

So I prayed, "Lord, show me a place that you want me to go." I tried churches all over the city, but most of them seemed the same. I would go in and sit there for awhile and two songs would be sung, someone would be called upon to say a prayer. It always seemed a rather meaningless one. The announcements would be given and someone would sing a solo. Then the minister would give a sermon with three or four points which never seemed to indicate that there was a real life relationship with the Lord or that we could expect miracles and conquer the powers of darkness.

I would be dejected. *Somewhere, somehow, I thought within my soul, there must be those that believe in a dynamic, living and vital Christ.* When an altar call would be given, one or two would come forward for salvation or no one at all. We'd be dismissed in prayer and go home just to sit and wait for another service where nothing would happen. This went on day after day.

I looked around, and it seemed that most people in the churches attended to see how beautifully they could dress or to show off their furs or their new clothes. They'd glance around to see if people were noticing.

The churches had to be beautiful. This had to be right, that had to be right, and the presence of God seemed so far away. I couldn't understand this. I cried to the Lord to lead me where I could meet someone who could teach me the depth of Jesus Christ and the power of His Spirit.

One day I was reading the paper and saw an article about a meeting in a stadium where all sorts of things were going on. The article reported that people were healed: goiters disappeared, cancer left them, and short legs were lengthened. It was called a *revival* meeting. I thought, *The stadium isn't a church. You can*

*go to a stadium anytime. That's where thousands
of people go to see ball games. Surely people would
not come there to show off their nice clothes.
I've got to go there and see what's going on.
Although perhaps I won't understand everything
I'm hearing—I want to go and find out what this
revival is all about.*

That was in December, 1958. It was an open-air
campaign and the weather was cold. I put on
a pair of slacks and dressed very warmly. I can
remember as I left the door of the apartment
I paused for a moment, closed my eyes and said
to Jesus, "Jesus, I want tonight to see your power.
Please let me find more of You." I'd never prayed
like this before, but I had such a longing in my
heart to know the deeper things of God, to be
able to live above sorrow and circumstances, to
live in the heights of God's blessing, victory and
power.

I remember that night very clearly. It was
the United Campaign being held in the South
China Stadium. There was a minister there from
the United. States. What an experience to hear
the message of the power of the Spirit of God!
He proclaimed that there is victory and that He
can flood our lives and our beings and give us
power to witness. He can heal our diseases, cure
the lame, heal the blind, cause us to leap for joy,
give us insights into His Word, speak to us through
His Word and His Spirit. How I longed and my
heart burned for this!

After the service there were many that went
forward to receive Jesus Christ as their Savior
or to receive healing. I can remember witnessing
to a woman who went forward and I saw with

my own eyes her goiter disappear as hands were laid upon her and people were praying to God for a miracle to happen—and it did.

After the closing of this special campaign, an Evangelistic Center was started in downtown Hong Kong, and I worked there as a secretary for two years. I experienced the joy of seeing people saved and healed, and all kinds of things happening!

One night after a Wednesday night prayer service a special call was given. How I desired to have that relationship with the Spirit of God and to know in my own life power and victory over sin and Satan. With my whole body trembling I went forward. I *had* to have this same experience of the power of God. A lady missionary was there also at the front to help me. I was told the steps that I was to take to receive the Holy Spirit. I was not to cling to my sin, I had to yield everything to God. So I confessed my sin and God cleansed my soul. As I did this, the Spirit of God fell upon me and gave me a love for those who had persecuted me and abused me. My heart longed for the Japanese and the Communists to know Jesus. I yielded all to Christ that night. I just asked Jesus to baptize me with His Holy Spirit, to fill me with His power. I can remember the joy and the feeling of the Spirit of God bathing me with His cleansing. I looked heavenward and the Spirit of God began speaking through me. The joy of praying in this new heavenly language was overwhelming!

I knew then what real freedom was. My soul had been set free by the Spirit of God and joy flooded my life! After this happened to me, I began examining my money handling. This was my first job in a free country, and my starting salary was 150 Hong Kong dollars. That wasn't much, but no matter how low my salary, all I wanted to do was to serve the Lord and to learn and experience and prepare myself for further use by Him.

When I walked out of China I left like a beggar. I didn't have anything and I had lost everything. My mother-in-law at that time gave me four bars of gold worth $1,200 in Hong Kong money. That was all the property I had plus my three children. There were five mouths for me to feed and at that time no income. The bars of gold were important to me, especially as security in case of emergency. I always thought: *If worse comes to worse I can sell the four bars of gold and get money to sustain us.* Until today my in-laws never knew what I had done with the bars of gold.

When the Americans came over to the South Stadium in the beginning of 1959 they were talking about needing money to help the crusade. It took a lot of money to rent the stadium and to pay for all the literature that they had been giving away for over three weeks. As they told about their needs I felt awful. I didn't have money to give because I didn't have any income. I said, "Lord, here I am, but I don't have anything to give You."

Then the Lord reminded me that I had four bars of gold hidden in the bank and that I should give these to Him. I argued with Him that I could not give it because this was all the money I had for an emergency. "Lord, this is everything. If I give it to You, I will have nothing," I said.

141

After reasoning this way I had such unrest in my heart, and I kept thinking over and over if I didn't give it to the Lord then it would show that I really didn't love Him.

I hadn't realized then that giving was a part of worship. The Lord gave me a verse in Malachi 3:10: " 'Bring the whole tithe into the storehouse, so that there may be food in My house, and test Me now in this,' says the Lord of hosts, 'if I will not open for you the windows of heaven, and pour out for you a blessing until there is no more need.' "

I said, "Now I know I must obey You and if I do my soul will be blessed by what I do." I kept asking Him and He kept revealing to me how these people had sacrificed for Him. I should just forget about my own situation because He was there to meet all my needs. I should put myself in His trust and love.

I went to the bank and took two bars of gold out of the box and slipped them into my bag. *There goes $800 which is far too much for me to give,* I thought. I still didn't realize the true meaning of obedience. It doesn't matter how much one gives to the Lord, but how we yield it. So finally I came home and the Lord said to me, "Nora, that's not what I told you to do. I don't need your money, but you do need My blessing." After I had given the two bars of gold I didn't feel His blessing, and I said, "Why don't I feel the blessing and the peace and joy? I gave you two! The other two, God, I must keep for emergencies." God replied, "Nora, you don't need to set any aside, you have me for all your needs.

Haven't I told you time and time again that I will supply all your needs?"

Then I felt so ashamed. He had brought me out of Red China, delivered me from the Japanese and had even given me back my life. I thought of the dark, dark night before the firing squad, how I stood there in fear and then in peace as I heard the count, one—two—three—fire. I heard the crack of the guns and I stood there alive. Not one bullet hit me.

Now here I was holding back two bars of gold from Jesus. I went to the bank and took out the other bars of gold. I can't describe the peace and relief that my heart felt as I placed them in the offering. In all these years that I have been traveling with my children in the United States the Lord has given me food for my family as He did long ago for the children of Israel.

I didn't have my husband to support me financially and I was taking care of three children and my mother, who was now seventy-two years old. Every day I saw the miracles of God supplying us from Heaven. Not one day have I had to worry. His mercy, His grace, and His peace are always there.

It's just like the five fishes and the two loaves. When they started to break them they were blessed with more than they could eat. If you are always going to keep something like a vial of perfume and never break the seal, you will never smell the beautiful perfume, nor will it ever spread. I learned that day to give of my material possessions.

Rich people may not be concerned with just

four bars of gold, because it really wasn't much. But I thank the Lord for the testing to see if I would give Him all that I had. How thankful I am that I did obey Him and that I learned this very important lesson. He kept His promise and has blessed me all these years more than I could ask or think. Suffering—sorrow—anguish? Yes, those have all been true, but so has Jesus. God has blessed me day by day and placed me on a mountaintop of joy.

Chapter Fifteen
THE DIVORCE

I have prayed much from the very start of this book about this chapter. There could be a lot of reactions, and it could even destroy my ministry, but even so I want to share it. I believe my experience can be useful to anyone who reads these pages.

Today there are many people getting married —only to have marriage end in divorce. Perhaps if I relate to them my suffering, God can use it to help them. I am going to be honest before God.

My romance began many years ago when

I was just a young girl. A young man from Hong Kong came to the same university that I was attending. I was a young girl from Shanghai, and when I saw this handsome young man, I was attracted by his outward appearance. He was tall and handsome. I never for a moment thought it mattered what he was really like—only that he was good looking.

I was possessed with the thought of him being my husband. I was a Christian, but it never entered my mind to find out what God would have me to do about this boy. There were people who tried to give me advice, but I would listen to no one. I was blinded by his looks.

I want to be free in sharing with you this stage in my life and to confess my weakness. I wanted him for my husband, no matter what the cost. Nothing was going to stand in my way—God or anyone.

I was proud thinking of us together because I was only a junior and he was a senior. I had planned to meet him by going to the library or to the study hall—every chance I could get I would take. I made up any kind of excuse to talk to him and be near him.

There was something strange about him. He had such a sad and melancholy spirit. His feelings were so negative about many things, but I had such a deep love for him that I didn't concern myself with his problems. I convinced myself that he had none, even though I knew he did. I thought that if I gave him love that would overcome all these feelings and change him. *If I can only get him to marry me everything will be all right,* I thought.

I really loved this man, and even when we were suffering under the attacks of Communism I would have given anything for him. When he would come home after being persecuted I would rub his back and wash his feet; anything to comfort him. When we didn't have any food I would run out into the street to buy something for him at the black market. I would have starved to feed him. I even attempted to sacrifice my own life so that he could be released from Red China. None of these sacrificial acts appeased my sin. The secret that I am going to share now is not even known to my family.

My husband and I were *legally* married on July 1, 1955. The reason I say *legally* was because I was pregnant before we were married. That is the secret that has been in my heart that I have not shared with anybody. I am sure that is one of the reasons for my suffering during this marriage. I thought he would learn to love and stop hating me if I had a baby, and that everything would be wonderful. It breaks my heart today when I see the abuse of sex all over the world. Young people today are practicing free love and thinking sex is the answer to all their problems. Girls are not cautious about their relationships with their boyfriends. Let me warn you that no one, absolutely no one, should have sexual relations with anyone except in the bonds of holy matrimony. I know many will not understand this, but I trust the Spirit of God will urge parents to warn their children to steer clear of immorality like a plague. It is important not to have relations before marriage even with your intended husband. The code is strong that a bride must be a virgin to her husband. Otherwise the rest of your life the woman cannot hold up her head and will be ostracized from the family. Today women getting pregnant before marriage is not news, and perhaps to many of you this might seem like trivia. I suffered for nine years and it's a horrible story, but I feel the Spirit of God would have me share it with you.

After our marriage things went quite well until the death of my father when my mother came to stay with us. My husband went into a rage, threw cups against the wall, and slapped me on the face. This was the first time I had seen him do this; his violence frightened me. I didn't realize anything was wrong with him and I couldn't quite understand. I rationalized that this must be a reaction from the oppression he was suffering under the Communists. "When he escapes and we are reunited," I told myself, "everything will be wonderful." And he did escape and get out of Red China.

The first night after my arrival in Hong Kong from China, of course, I had been pregnant for twelve months. I was fat, heavy, and sick. All he could say was: "Why didn't you bring the safety deposit key for my Bank of Red China?" He complained over and over. I was so happy that I had arrived that I didn't understand why he kept nagging at me because of the key. He hit me and told me I should have brought the key out of China. I tried to explain to him that the soldiers took the ring off my finger and would not let me escape with a key. I started to cry, but I dared not cry aloud because my mother-in-law was upstairs and all would hear, and they would discover the tragedy that was taking place. I was tired, sick, and ready to give birth, but I didn't receive any comfort from him. From the very beginning of our friendship, our love and our marriage were not on a solid foundation and there was little harmony between us.

I didn't realize that a spiritual battle was going on in him. The man I loved and had sacrificed my life for shouldn't treat me like this!

After the baby was born and I was working at an evangelistic center in Hong Kong, my husband was angry with me. He would kick me out of bed, because I worked in the church. His abuse didn't let up when I wore the plaster cast on my left leg. With the cast on I wasn't able to move or work; he never offered to help me.

I went to work to help support our family as we didn't have enough money. I had two jobs at one time and tried to help save more money to get ahead. Sometimes he would take my paycheck away from me—and then beat me. I couldn't understand it. When I went to bed at night I poured out my heart to the Lord. Perhaps if I hadn't been married to such a mean man, and had a very sweet husband instead, I never would have been close to the Lord. It was hard to say, but I was drawing closer to Jesus when my loved one made me suffer. I guess that's what counted.

I was very disappointed, and started to realize that I had suffered under the Japanese, I had suffered under the Communists, and now I was suffering under my husband. But I had three little ones and I couldn't do anything to protest. They were small and needed a mother and father. I didn't want to see the family broken up, and I didn't have any choice but to endure. I can remember how my husband would wake up in the middle of the night; if he couldn't sleep he would not allow me to sleep. He would force me to sit on a chair while he poured hot water out of a cup over me. Then he would take a lighted cigarette and burn me with it in the middle of the night.

What could I do? As an American woman you can go out and call the police, but that's not the Chinese culture. Of course I dared not tell anyone. For this type of family saving face is very important. We would all lose face if it was learned that my husband was treating me like this.

There's no chance of escape in a Chinese family. Sometimes we would drive up to the mountains and then he would open up the door and say he wanted to push me out of the car. I can remember one night he took me there and told me to get out of the car. We were walking and he said, "I'm going to get in the car and leave you here." It was winter and it was cold. And he laughed and said, "Stay here and freeze." I asked the Lord over and over again, "What have I done wrong?" Now I am suffering from all these things and I couldn't understand it. I knelt down and begged him to take me home with Him because I was so scared that I would have to stay there overnight in the mountains and I would freeze to death. Someone would kill me. The Lord overruled in all these things. There was no experience He didn't see me through and I praise His holy name.

In 1965 we moved from the apartment back

into the old house. The people who were living on the ground floor moved out and we moved in. Before this, my husband had beaten me up only twice a year. Later it was four times a year, then once a month, once a week. By 1965 he tried to beat me up almost every day, then twice a day. It became more and more frequent. People would ask me about my bruises and I would be afraid to say anything. I covered up what was going on; I didn't want people to know. It was unheard of in the Chinese culture to ever think of a divorce. When he began to beat me regularly every night he said it was because he had lost money. Then he would say to me, "No, you stole it," and would slap my face. He used his shoe to hit me on the chest until I started to vomit blood. My head would get so painful that it felt like it was going to crack. I went to the doctor for X-rays and found out that I was swollen inside. I didn't have anywhere to turn but to Jesus.

This abuse went on for many years until such a depression hit me that I wanted to kill myself. I did not know that the Lord could permit these things to happen, and that I would later be able to share this experience with the women of Las Vegas who also suffer mentally and physically from their husbands.

We became such an unhappy family. My husband didn't change from evil to good, but just got worse. As I told you before, I worked for the social welfare office and I earned $600 a month. I always thought if I earned a lot of money we could have happiness at home. But then I thought it would be better to give up the money and wait on my husband; maybe then things would change. So after I quit my job and stayed home. I waited on him every minute of my waking hours. That was the biggest mistake I could have made, because in fact I couldn't change him at all.

I still remember the first week after I resigned that my mother had another attack and wasn't feeling well. I felt that I should call the doctor but didn't because I wasn't working and didn't have the money. I asked my maid if she could loan me $50 in Hong Kong money. I told her I needed the doctor to come out to see my mother. The doctor came and I paid him. I was upset because Mom was sick—when suddenly my husband came home and said he had lost $100 from his pocket. I must have been the one who stole his money! That happened at four-thirty. At five o'clock he slapped my face and hit me on the chest with his shoes. I had pain and went into the bathroom and vomited blood.

I picked up the phone and called my mother-in-law. That was the first time after all these years that I had ever shared anything with her. I told her that my husband had kicked me and she said he could never have done anything like that. She told me I was crazy. Now I felt worse than ever. I couldn't say a thing. I thought, *Well, if that's true I would rather die than to live like this.*

When I think about it now what I went through seems very unnecessary. There were so many things that I could have done, but I lost interest in everything. I said to myself that I had better die, because I didn't know where to turn. My children were little. We were Chinese and didn't practice divorce. My husband was abusing me physically and I couldn't take any more. I had been working on one job during the day and another one in the evening to earn more money. Still I couldn't satisfy him. The results were so disappointing that one day, as if an evil spirit took hold of me, something came over me and I said, "I'm going to die." I was living on the ninth floor of an apartment—actually what you Americans would call the tenth floor and it was a thirteen-story building. I ran to the top of the building and looked for a place to jump off the roof. This was the saddest part of my life. My oldest son Paul, who was only five years old, saw me run to the top of the building and ran after me. He used his little hand to hold me back while he begged me not to jump.

I listened to my son and went back down to our rooms. When my husband found out he got worse. Then he tried to lock me up in his room; he forced me to take medicine, tied me to the bed, and even took me to see a psychiatrist. I'm not against psychiatry, but some of the doctors are hard to believe. I felt something was wrong with myself, so I went to see a specialist hoping he would help me find a solution to my problems. I insisted on going to the public hospital sponsored by the Hong Kong government. I trusted those doctors and I didn't think anyone would cheat me.

I loved my children, and wondered what impression all this was making on them. Of course, the baby was too small to understand what was going on. Ruth was young too, but Paul knew. He would use his little hands time and time again to pull on me, to save me from death. Just as those little hands reached out to me in no man's land, so they were reaching out to me now. The Lord had prepared Paul to intercede so that I would not jump. If he had not been there I would have jumped long ago. But the Lord has mercy; He knew that I was suffering intensely yet He had a purpose in it which I didn't understand until later.

During these several months of terrible persecution I just didn't care for my life anymore. I didn't wash my face unless I was almost forced to. I never drank tea or water until I was made to swallow it. My mind was acting normally and I knew what was going on, but I was so sad and the world seemed so cruel that I just didn't care. People laughed at me, mocked me. They brought up the fact that I was adopted and suggested that there was mental illness in my real ancestry.

I began to understand about the world, that appearances were not what they seemed to be. I was comforted by many people with about as much help as Job got from his friends. They would say, "There must be something wrong with her. That's the reason she has suffered so hard."

It got so bad that I submitted to many things. A private doctor even gave me electric shock treatments three times for $100, each time to find out if there was something wrong with me. During the divorce proceedings my husband introduced to court the possibility of taking away my children from me and accused me of being a mental case. When things came out like this I really understood the cruelty of human beings, how they point at you behind your back. I wasn't a mental case at all.

I thank the Lord that the senior specialist in the hospital didn't give me any medicine. He didn't think I needed any. What I needed was encouragement, he believed, and I was released from the hospital. The private doctor wanted to put me in a private hospital in Hong Kong for a few days. They all looked at me as if I were a freak.

It was hard for me to accept the stares and jibes of my friends. I knew they thought there was something wrong with my mind. I had such a heartache that I couldn't share with anybody. That's why I was so depressed. Now I really understand depression because I have gone through it. I hated the world. I was forced to take medicine which I knew would make me unable to think. I would fight against submitting to the dose and would be hit violently by my husband as he forced it down my throat.

Then I realized, by the Word of God, that this was a spiritual battle I was fighting. I tried to exercise authority. I would say, "In the name of Jesus leave me alone." I just kept hoping God would end this terrible thing soon. I knew that He wouldn't forsake me, and that He would care for me, His daughter, and of course He would always love me.

I prayed for all these things myself. Finally one day I was given direction from God which I followed. In obedience I came to the United States, and traveled from the East coast to the West coast. Finally I found a place in Hayward, California, to live.

I thought that my husband would be pleased because I had arranged everything for him so that he could come to the States. I went back to Hong Kong in September of 1966, even though he kept saying it would be better to have a divorce. He was drinking heavily at this time, and was almost constantly at the bottle.

Our entire family migrated to the United States when I left Hong Kong this time. From then on my life in America once more became nothing but mental and physical torture, night after night. Again I thought that I could somehow get him to change. I pleaded with the Lord to show me what to do or where to go. "Something, please, Lord."

The threats on my life continued every night, and he said he would kill me and take away the children. I was reduced to skin and bones and was a nervous wreck. Finally I was advised by a lawyer, and had confirmation from God, that I should leave my husband or he would truly kill me someday. This was the hardest time of my life; my escape from Red China seemed small in comparison to the way I felt when I left my husband. One day I took the children out of school and got on a plane from Oakland to Los Angeles. That was in February, 1967. My oldest child was eleven, my daughter was ten, and the youngest was eight and a half. I knelt down in the airport and cried to the Lord, "What have I done wrong? I don't want these children to suffer, but I don't know which way to turn. I don't have any friends or relatives, God, I only have you." Then the Lord told me to go to Denver. I had met a couple from Denver in Hong Kong in 1958. I would try to see them.

There was lots of snow in Denver when we arrived, and we checked into a motel and tried to find this couple. They had just moved, I knew that much. Finally I went to the police and they located my friends. They treated us as if we were their own family. How many times I have thanked God for the Fords!

I didn't know what to do from day to day, but I knew that the Lord was going to care for us. We soon returned to California on Valentine's day. The separation was finally granted and my former husband promised to send a check for child support; none ever came. I couldn't understand why, but I knew that Jesus would tell me when I met Him face to face.

I flew to Las Vegas. This time the lawyer didn't want me to take the children. I learned that he thought I was a mental case. My husband tried to give the lawyer a false impression that I had been in a mental hospital. They soon found out that there was nothing wrong with me, and realized I was being persecuted by him.

The divorce became final on May 24, 1967. I started my new life as an evangelist declaring God's goodness and mercy.

I traveled for five years sharing the forgiveness, the blessing, the mercy, and the power of God my Father, Jesus my Savior, and the Holy Spirit my Comforter.

Cook in Las Vegas

Chapter Sixteen

THE GREATNESS OF
HIS POWER

In January of 1960 I fell and hurt myself so severely that I was in a cast for months. One night as I was laying there praying, the Lord gave me a vision. I saw myself sharing Christ to an audience of green eyes and blue eyes. I thought, *These aren't my people. They're from the other side of the world.* I saw myself standing in front of thousands of people and I thought, *This can't be a vision. This must be a dream. God could never use me.* Now I realize that was the day the Lord called me to the United States from Hong Kong to begin my ministry of testifying and sharing Christ.

I had lived in Hong Kong from 1958 to 1966. Never in all those years had I spoken to people in a group meeting about the gospel, and I had never publicly given a testimony. All those years the Lord was testing me, trying me, refining me. Later on when He called me to share a testimony I could give evidence of His power within my own life.

Many times in private I would use whatever extra money I had to invite people to my home or bring them to church. Then I would share Christ with them. But I never thought that the Lord could use me to minister from the pulpit. As the secretary in the Evangelistic Center in Hong Kong I heard great teachers who would come over and share the Word of God. I learned so much from them. I learned how to walk close to God, to believe in His miracles, and to lift my hands for His power. How thankful I am that He prepared me for the ministry! My heart became burdened for my people, for my loved ones, for my country of China. I realized that in this vast land there are over 300 million children who have never heard of Jesus. Almost two-thirds of the world's population is concentrated in the East.

I'll never forget the night that Reverend Bill Thornton wanted me to come to his church and speak. I didn't speak very good English then and I expected to have an interpreter. But at the last moment he announced to the people that I was there and I was going to speak. "Lord," I prayed, "what am I going to do?" He said, "It's not what *you* are going to do. It's what *I* am going to do. Nora, just yield yourself to me and I will speak." So I got up on the platform in obedience and the first night the Lord spoke through me and the people were very moved by what I was saying. Then I went to Denver, Chicago, Pittsburgh, and visited Kathryn Kuhlman for forty-six days. I went to Los Angeles and shared my testimony of deliverance on her television program.

I still didn't want to be an evangelist. All this time I was searching for answers: where was I going to live? what kind of life was I going to have? I certainly didn't want to be in the ministry. It just wasn't my way of life. I would work any place for Him, but not preach.

After my divorce I was so broken that I thought, *Now God can never use me. I'm a disgrace.* Then I realized that His forgiveness endures forever. He had called me to a life of suffering so that I could share now with others the joy of forgiveness and deliverance. I began speaking for the Lord, and for five years I traveled from city to city, and from church to church. The more I have spoken the more I have felt His anointing upon me.

Soon the Lord told me that I was to return to my people in Taiwan, the Republic of China. He spoke to me in such a clear way. I told Him, "God, I'm afraid to go back even to Taiwan. I don't know many people there. Who is going to ask me to speak?" The Lord again told me to go. I said, "Lord, if I go and no one asks me to speak, can I just forget it and come back home?" I had no choice but to obey.

I was upset and I thought, *If I don't go the Lord will be unhappy with me.* I must leave at once. I told my daughter Ruth to skip school and come home to help me pack. The distance from the school to home was just about five minutes by car. I was so busy that morning I asked one of my friends to go to the school and pick her up. If I'd realized what was going to happen that day I would never have asked her to come home.

About five minutes after my daughter left the school, I was waiting for them to come home when the phone rang. It was a call from the hospital telling me that there had been a car accident, my daughter was unconscious, and that I should come to the hospital immediately. I was stunned and shocked. "Lord, now what has happened?" I asked.

When I got to the hospital Ruth was in the emergency room. A man came over and told me that he was from the police department. He then showed me the side of the car where my daughter had been sitting. The car was a total loss. A great fear gripped my heart about the condition in which I'd find my daughter. After about three hours of waiting, walking back and forth and repenting, I asked the Lord to forgive me for being disobedient. This disobedience had made my daughter suffer. God's mercy is more than I could ever describe. The wait was tiring and the hospital seemed to smell like a fish market with its odors of medicine. My daughter finally was brought out. The nurse told me they had given her X-rays and not one bone in her body had been broken. Bits of broken glass were all over her, but not one place on her body was cut. She didn't have a scratch.

My daughter talked to me through her tears. "Mother, how come you don't want to preach the gospel? How come you don't want to go? You didn't ask the Lord to protect us, but He did anyway. There is no sense in your staying home. If you don't do the Lord's work God won't be pleased. Mom, He can protect you wherever you go. Please go and preach to the Chinese people in Taiwan.''

It was dreadful that my daughter had to share these things with me. I was so ashamed that I hadn't wanted to yield myself to the Lord and be His servant and go to my people! After all the great miracles that had happened in my life, I still had a heart that would not obey. I said to the Lord right there in the hospital, "Lord, I'm going to Taiwan to preach the gospel there for you. Whatever you tell me to do from this day on I will do it.''

I cried and prayed most of the night. I felt like a child coming back to the Lord again. Sometimes when we tell our children to obey us or to do as they are told they say, "Oh Mom, we're busy." This hurts our feelings. Well, I had done the same thing. I had hurt God's feelings. I had nailed Jesus to the cross again by my rejection. I didn't appreciate Him and I really didn't want to be used by Him.

In March I went to Taiwan. There were many different types of people living on the island. There were some native Taiwanese and many others from mainland China. Some had moved there before the Communists took over, and had lived there for twenty years or more.

It was hard for me to go to this land and ask to have a meeting. I was a single woman and didn't know any of the pastors. When the Lord called me to do this He had to go ahead and prepare the way. He recalled to my mind that ten years prior I had met Reverend Lee. "Lord, what am I going to do?" I asked. His reply was, "You just call Reverend Lee and the revival will start from there."

So I called Reverend Lee and he came to the hotel lobby. I told him the Lord wanted me to preach the gospel. He said, "Who are you that you can push yourself like this and think that you should preach the Gospel?" I told him if he prayed and I prayed we could see how the Lord would speak to our hearts. He began to think, *How can I refuse her?* The more he thought, the stranger it seemed to him that I should approach him. He felt compelled to say, "Nora, okay. You can start your revival next week and we will hold the meetings from Tuesday until Sunday. We have one weekend to advertise."

The first Tuesday night there were only about fifty people at the meeting. I was somewhat disappointed. However I shared the burden of my heart that the Lord was still alive and about my escape from Red China. The power of the Spirit of God came down that night and touched a man who was in charge of an orphanage. I didn't know, but he had serious problems with his eyes and had had many operations. He couldn't see, but that night the Lord miraculously restored his vision. He went to the doctor the following day and had his eyes checked. The doctor said, "Well, I don't know what's happened. You have almost perfect vision."

The man, named C. P. Ying, came back the following night and gave his testimony. On

Thursday there were almost 600 people. That night people were healed of all sorts of diseases. It was even hard to keep track. Many people knelt down and gave their hearts to Jesus, and the Spirit of the Lord did marvelous things.

Then the Lord said to me, "You have to close your meetings." I asked, "Why, Lord? So many things are happening. Isn't this what you called me here to do, to share my testimony?" He said, "I want you to move from here to the stadium." I should have the next two meetings on Saturday and Sunday, which happened to be Easter Sunday. People were amazed that this woman who was obviously Chinese acted like one who was half-Chinese and half-American. They felt like I had become an American girl so independent when suddenly I wanted to rent the stadium and take the meetings from the church there. The Lord said, "I gave you 600 who came to this meeting today, but I will give you 6,000 at the stadium. You must only obey and walk with Me."

I questioned this leading. "But God, how am I going to get the money and get the people to come to hear me? That's tomorrow." And He answered, "It is by My Spirit and My Spirit alone that many people will come to the stadium." When I heard the Lord saying this I thought I was kidding myself because these big revivals had to have trained workers and months of preparation. God again said, "Nora, if you do it in My name, it will be done."

So the next morning Reverend Lee and a few other church organizers had a breakfast with me. Everybody there was doing his best to discourage me and I was worried about continuing the revival without preparation. But the Lord told me not to listen to anyone but Him and He said, "Nora, you go and rent the stadium."

When I told them that the Lord wanted me to rent the stadium they said, "Well, it's impossible. We have a ball game going on during those days." I told them, "But God told me He wanted me to use this place." I discovered that when you speak in the authority of God, people will listen to you. The manager couldn't say anything to refuse me because God was moving on his heart. He said we could use the stadium on Saturday evening and Sunday afternoon which were exactly the right times for the people to come to the crusade. We didn't have ushers or personal workers and this was our weakest point.

Soon God spoke to the precious students of the Wesley High School and they willingly offered and gave their time to the service of the Lord.

Saturday night at the revival people were healed—and the crippled and lame walked. A man who didn't even know the Lord came to the meeting and was healed. His name was Wong. I was moved greatly as I looked at the multitude who were so hungry, and listened to them sing and worship the Lord. How I longed to see these people restored to the Mainland and to have their country back. I didn't know how long these poor souls could suffer without their land. I asked the Lord to help me to minister to them in the exact way that would meet their needs. I thank the Lord that on Easter Sunday He gave me a message: Jesus Christ was still alive in the world today to minister to people's needs and that the Spirit of

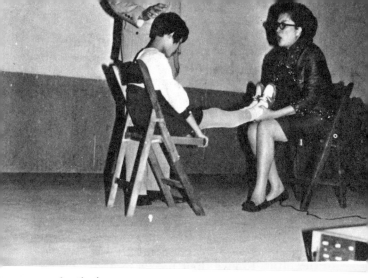

Nora prays for the lame.

They brought the sick to Jesus.

God is the same Spirit that fell on the world on the Day of Pentecost.

People were saved and healed and I could hardly understand the power and the why of these things that were happening. Now as I look back I realize that after President Nixon went to Red China he said America was going to reduce the support and help the people in Nationalist China. Free China was put out of the United Nations and Red China was given its seat. These poor souls needed to know the reality of the living Christ and the Holy Spirit that could empower them to go on. It was in the wake of this unexpected and unbelievable crisis that people came this Easter Day, to the altar, to give their hearts to Jesus. God did as He said because overnight we went from 600 to 4,000 and then to 6,000 with little publicity. The gospel moved on them and the people were hungry.

Then another miracle was about to take place. As I was closing the meeting on Easter Sunday the people crowded forward to speak to me and to touch me, to have me lay hands on them to pray with them. Towards the end of the service, as they tried to get near me I was pushed off the platform. I twisted my ankle and tore some of the tendons in my foot. I could hardly walk. I continued, however, to help Reverend Lee baptize these people. When I walked out of the water my feet could not carry me. I was taken by taxi to the hospital and examined. I was told that my ankle was twisted and that my tendons were torn. It would be weeks, according to the doctor, before I would be able to walk on it without pain.

I said, "Lord, after all these people have come here and have been healed, You mean to tell me

You are going to send me away in a wheelchair? That will mean all of Your glory will come to mean zero." The pain was unbearable.

I called back to the United States to a very dear brother in Christ and told him I had an accident. He said, "Nora, I knew it." In spite of the sixteen hours difference in time between the United States and Taiwan, at the exact moment that I had been hurt he had seen a vision that I had been hit by these hundreds of devils beating me down. He prayed in the name of Jesus for my deliverance. Finally every demon left me alone and he felt peace. He knew I would be healed.

There was a lady who was visiting me the following morning at the Grand Hotel Taipei and I asked her if she would pray for my healing. She said she didn't know how. So I said, "You lay your hands on me and I'll pray." As she placed her hands on my feet she opened her mouth and said, "Lord, You sent Nora over here to do Your work. And now she has to go home in a wheelchair. Lord, this isn't right. Let your name be glorified. Please touch her foot."

As she was praying the power of God came down from heaven and released every pain in my foot. Immediately I was able to walk out of the hotel. How thankful I was that once again God proved Himself to me before my own people in Taiwan. I realized as never before "the greatness of His power."

Chapter Seventeen
FOR THOSE TEARS

"Hello, Mr. Dudley? This is Nora Lam. Do you remember me?"

These were the words I heard as I answered my telephone early one morning in my office.

"Of course I remember our meeting in San Bernadino. May I help you with something?" I replied.

"Mr. Dudley, it's nine o'clock in the morning. I'm wide awake. And perhaps you're going to be amazed at what I'm going to share with you, but I want you to know that I've prayed before making this phone call. I can only say that if it is truly of God, you'll be able to accept what I'm going to share."

She then related to me the story of the old Chinese man who had come to visit her as a child. I'm sure you'll remember that story as it was told in the pages you have already read. "This morning," she continued, "after almost thirty years he came to see me again. In my vision he showed me Free China. You were on my right side, and on my left was another man whom I do not know. He beckoned us to come to the Chinese people. And then I saw a door opened into Taiwan that in turn opened into the vast country of Red China. Mr. Dudley, we're to go there and tell these people about Jesus. Do you understand that?"

"Well, not really," was my reply. "But I'll pray about it."

Then she said, "God bless you, good-bye," and hung up the phone.

I sat at my desk for a few moments thinking that I just had a dream. That conversation just couldn't have taken place. As the pressures of the day mounted I pushed the conversation out of my mind, I suppose thinking of it as somewhat of a hoax.

Several months later I was in the state of California. I went to the home of Mr. Dewey Lockman, head of the Lockman Foundation, and there he played for me a tape of a sermon given by a minister in California. The tape was on China, and it related how the Bamboo Curtain had fallen on that country not once, but five times, and missionaries were driven out.

The tape stirred my soul like it has never

been stirred before, and I had for the first time a vision for the hundreds of millions dying without Christ in China.

I decided then that I would take a flight to San Jose and visit Nora Lam. After I boarded the plane I had a very unusual experience during my prayer time. The thought came to me that if I would pray aloud it would be in Chinese. However I suppressed the idea and did not give way to the moving of the Spirit. Later as I arrived at Miss Lam's home and we discussed the possibility of a book, I told her we should pray to seek God's will. Once again as I was praying the thought came to me that if I would give voice to it, I could pray in Chinese. Once again I suppressed the Spirit's movement upon me. As Nora was praying the Spirit said to me, "If you will not speak it, the least you can do is write it." I lifted my pen and wrote down phonetically four sentences with the tonal marks, realizing that for the first time I was putting to practical use the knowledge I had learned at the Summer Institute of Linguistics sponsored by the Wycliffe Bible Translators. This knowledge had lain dormant for over twenty-two years.

When Nora Lam had prayed I turned to her saying, "Do these marks make any sense to you?"

Of course her reply was, "No. But can you say what's on the paper."

"I believe so." And very slowly I pronounced the words that I had written. They read: "And God had spoken saying, 'The door I have opened no one will shut. And I will go before and prepare the way. Go into Tainan, Kaochung, and Taitung with Sung Neng Yee.' " (Sung Neng Yee was Nora Lam's Chinese name which I had never heard.)

The family's mouths fell open with amazement, for I had spoken Mandarin Chinese. Just to make sure, I repeated these words to another Chinese person and he validated the exact translation.

Now my heart was stirred as never before. Perhaps that telephone conversation *was* truth, and God would prepare a way for us to go to Tainan and later into Red China.

Months passed and I began working on this book. In the mail one day to my surprise I received a round trip ticket from Chicago to Taipei, Taiwan. Nora Lam was already there and had begun her meetings. I joined the staff in the city of Khaochung.

We gave testimony of Jesus Christ and sang to the glory of God. There were ministers with whom we met and ministered to, telling them of the baptism of the Holy Spirit and the power of God that is available today. It was interesting to see how God began to move. I had never in my life experienced anything like it. As you look at the photos you can easily see the multitudes of people God brought to Himself in those few short days.

My heart was stirred and at unrest in the city of Tainan, for this was a city containing many temples of false gods. As we traveled down the road I saw two huge gold Buddhas at the entrance of a huge rubber factory. Then further down the street there were more gods and more temples. The nearer we got to the city, the more

Pastors come to learn of the power of the Holy Spirit.

Nora speaking in Taipei

佈道醫神大會盛況　台北中華體育文
一九七一年四月

Thousands respond to the invitation in Tainan.

They stream forward to declare their faith.

depressed and sickly we became. I realized for the first time in my life the awful terror and power of the living Satan.

The meetings began rather meagerly with perhaps 500 in attendance. But as the nights drew on and the power of God fell upon these people the numbers increased—until we had to rent the huge stadium in Tainan. Once again Miss Lam trusted God to send the people. They came. The Spirit of God ministered to them and they came forward by the thousands. I saw first hand: people delivered from disease, legs lengthened, deaf ears opened, the demon-possessed set free. I witnessed first hand the change in a Buddhist priest who had been bound by Satan for years, who had not been able to sleep soundly for over seven years because of the torment of demons. I heard him testify that Jesus was the Son of God, the living Christ, his Savior, and that he had been set free from the power of demons.

Many people today feel that God's power is limited. We can't expect miracles, they say, and we can't expect the multitudes to be delivered. I am thankful God permitted me to see and record by film the mighty outpouring of His Holy Spirit in Taiwan.

We went on to Taitung and once again we saw the mighty movement of God. I also met God's faithful few who through the years have been faithful in ministering there. I remember one such man by the name of Hue Man Shih, pastor of the Mandarin church in Taitung, a man in his eighties. The glory of God really shone through him; the burden for his people was great. He sacrificed like I've never seen anyone sacrifice before. His son is a very well-to-do man and as his father he could be living in comfort rather than the poverty he prefers in order to bring Jesus to the people of Taitung.

Many of the ministers in Kaohchung came over the mountains to be with us in Taitung. Among them was Pastor Andrew Chen, an Assembly of God minister, Reverend Tsay Kai Tarng, Reverend Pan Chung Chiey, and Reverend Yuan Tak Hui, all Presbyterians and so on. The fellowship was wonderful, and what a joy to see their hearts strengthened by what God was showing them. How wonderful it was to see these men of God lay hands on the sick, and pray for deliverance of the possessed.

God is alive and active. I'm so thankful that I was permitted to see this and to validate these things I've written in this book as true. There will be many skeptics among my readers, but I pray that God will enlighten your hearts to understand and to know that the Spirit of God is alive and is moving across the face of the earth, like a mighty wind. His voice will not be silenced.

As Nora Lam has told her story, it is our prayer that out of her suffering will come blessings to many.